The Martyrs of Legal Terrorism

A state sponsored Genocide.

RUDOLPH D'SOUZA

Made with ♡ on the Notion Press Platform

www.notionpress.com

Legal Disclaimer

This book is intended for informational and educational purposes only. It does not constitute legal advice. Readers are advised to consult with legal professionals for specific guidance on legal matters.

For permissions, inquiries, or media requests, please contact:

Printed in India

Dedication

To my son, **Glenn Shannon**,

My heart beats for you, even when my arms cannot reach you. I remember the day you were born—the first time I held you, your tiny fingers wrapped around mine, a bond that I thought would last forever. But that bond was torn apart, piece by piece, by a system that turned my love into a weapon against me. A child whose innocence was stolen, whose childhood was marked by the absence of a father's love. You grew up without knowing me, without the warmth of my embrace, or the guidance of my presence.

For thirteen years, I fought to be your father—through courtrooms filled with cold indifference, through judgments that mocked my plea, through a deposit of Rupees **10 lakhs (1 Million)** demanded just to see you **ONCE**, only to be turned away at the door. I fought not because I wanted to win, but because I wanted you to know that you were loved, that you had a father who would never stop trying to reach you. For thirteen long years, I fought tirelessly, through the labyrinth of legal battles, only to be met with cruelty and mockery. The system that should have protected us became a weapon of separation. Even when the courts granted me visitation, the walls of alienation remained impenetrable.

Your childhood was stolen—not just from you, but from me too. I missed your first steps, your first words, and the sound of your laughter. I missed the chance to tell you stories, to wipe your tears, to be the shield that protected you. You grew up in a world where I was erased, where you were told I didn't exist. But I exist, Glenn. I exist in every prayer I whisper for you, in every dream where I see your face, in every thought that wonders if you're safe, if you're happy, if you're loved.

This book is my love letter to you. It is the only way I can tell you that I never gave up, that I never stopped fighting, that I never stopped loving you. I pray that one day, you will read these words and know the truth—that you have always been my son, and I have always been your father.

May your life be filled with the love, peace, and joy that was stolen from us both.

Acknowledgments

This book is dedicated to the countless souls who fell victim to the scourge of **Legal Terrorism**—those who lost their lives, those who took their own life in despair, and those who were silenced by a system that failed them. Your real-life stories will not be forgotten. I bow my head in memory of the countless Voiceless men who lost their lives in silence—men who were unheard, unseen, and unspoken for. This book is dedicated to them—the voiceless who carried their pain quietly, pushed beyond their limits by circumstances they did not choose, and systems that failed them.

I also extend my deepest gratitude to the members of **MyNation Hope Foundation**, who stand as a beacon of hope and support for those battling this injustice. Your courage, resilience, and unwavering commitment to justice inspire this work.

To the families of these men—especially the parents, siblings, and friends who continue to fight for justice—your resilience and love are a beacon of hope in a world that often turns a blind eye. This book would not have been possible without your support and truth.

To every individual who has suffered in silence, this book is your voice. May it ignite change and bring an end to the darkness of legal oppression, Legal Terrorism and State sponsored Genocide.

I also wish to acknowledge the feminists, women's ministries, and women's NGOs whose unwavering support for gender-biased policies, societal division, legal injustices, Legal Terrorism against men and Genocide of men fueled my determination to write this book and shed light on these critical issues.

Special thanks to Sunita's for making me infamous with a 498A case that's dragged on for 25 years, taking the children away from me, and using their names to beg for money—this gem was born from that long, bitter journey.

Lastly, I thank every reader who dares to open their mind and heart to this conversation. In a world where narratives are often one-sided, your willingness to listen is the first step toward change.

This book is not an attack—it is a plea. A plea for justice, for empathy, and for a society that values all its voices equally, regardless of gender.

Let the unheard be heard.

With gratitude,

RUDOLPH DSOUZA

Author's Note

In writing "***The Martyrs of Legal Terrorism***,"
I felt compelled to shed light on a deeply troubling
issue that often remains obscured by societal biases:
the plight of men who find themselves ensnared in
legal systems that should protect them but instead
perpetuate injustice. This book chronicles the
harrowing experiences of those who, pushed to the
brink by relentless harassment under biased laws,
have tragically succumbed to the pressure to end
their lives.

These stories are not merely anecdotes; they are
powerful testaments to the systemic failures within
our judicial framework that leave many without
recourse. It is a painful truth that these men, many
of whom have been alienated from their families and
denied the ability to be present in their children's
lives, have faced insurmountable odds in their
struggles for justice.

I want to clarify that my intention is not to disparage
the feminist movement or to vilify the government
but to spotlight the necessity of balance and fairness
in our legal system. The ongoing demonization of
men in the name of empowerment has led to a
distortion of justice. This book is an honest attempt
to bring awareness to these pressing issues and to

advocate for a legal framework that genuinely
supports all individuals, regardless of gender.

It is my aspiration that the narratives within these
pages ignite a spark of awareness and empathy
among readers. I believe that by understanding these
injustices, we can cultivate a firestorm of advocacy
that demands reform and accountability. Together,
we can work toward a future where justice is not a
privilege for a select few but a fundamental right for
all.

Let this work serve as both a call to action and a
beacon of hope. Change is possible, Change is within
reach, and with every reader who embraces this
cause, we move closer to a world where justice is a
right, not a privilege, for everyone.

Table of Contents

Preface

The term "***Legal Terrorism***" was starkly highlighted when India's Supreme Court recognized how laws meant to protect women could become weapons of harassment. This book delves into the dark reality where protective legislation made for protection of women transforms into tools of extortion, harassment, and psychological warfare, leading countless innocent individuals to take their own lives.

The term "**Legal Terrorism**", coined by the Supreme Court of India, encapsulates a harrowing reality where laws designed to safeguard justice are perversely exploited to inflict suffering. This book sheds light on the systemic abuse of legal provisions, where women, police, lawyers, and even family court judges collude in a nexus of extortion and psychological torment, driving countless men to the brink of despair—and tragically, to suicide.

During my two decade-long research into this phenomenon, I witnessed how a complex nexus of corrupt officials, unethical legal practitioners, and manipulative individuals have twisted protective laws into instruments of torment. Just as anti-terror laws faced criticism for their misuse against minorities and political dissent, Women centric, domestic violence and other laws too have become weapons of oppression through their systematic abuse. Through meticulous research and heart-wrenching narratives, this work exposes how protective laws, intended to shield the vulnerable, have been weaponized against innocent individuals. The misuse of statutes such as domestic violence and dowry laws has created a vicious cycle of false accusations, financial exploitation, and emotional devastation. Police often turn a blind eye to due process, lawyers capitalize on the chaos, and family court judges, bound by outdated interpretations, perpetuate the cycle of injustice.

The stories documented here reveal a disturbing pattern where the machinery of justice - from law enforcement to courtrooms - becomes complicit in what can only be described as state-sanctioned harassment. The victims, predominantly men, and also his families. Old aged parents who have been falsely accused, face a calculated assault on their dignity, finances, and psychological well-being, often leading to tragic consequences.

This book aims to expose how, much like the misuse of anti-terror laws that led to prolonged detentions without trial, domestic laws have created a parallel system of persecution where accusations alone become tools of torture. Through extensive case studies and testimonials, I demonstrate how the very institutions meant to protect citizens have become instruments of harassment through a calculated nexus of corrupt stakeholders, like Police, Lawyers, Judges and women Organisations.

This is not merely about gender biases; it is about a systemic failure where the very pillars of justice have been corrupted. The stories of men who forced to commit suicide within these pages reveal how legal terrorism thrives in the shadows of collusion, where the accused are presumed guilty until proven innocent, and the burden of proof becomes an insurmountable mountain.

This work advocates for urgent systemic changes to prevent the weaponization of protective laws. The stories of those who succumbed to this legal terrorism, serve as both a memorial and a urgent call for reform.

My intent is not to undermine the importance of protective legislation but to expose its metamorphosis into a tool of oppression when wielded by unscrupulous elements. This book stands as testimony to those who fell victim to this systematic abuse and aims to catalyse much-needed reforms in our legal system.

The intent of this book is not to vilify women or undermine the importance of protective laws, but to highlight the urgent need for accountability and reform. It serves as a call to action to dismantle the nexus and to restore faith in the justice system.

Taking one's own life is an act of unimaginable despair, a final surrender that no soul undertakes lightly. For a man to reach such a precipice, he must have endured relentless torment—vilified by those he once loved, harassed by a society that turns a blind eye, and tortured by a legal system that should have been his refuge but instead became his oppressor.

Stripped of hope, his cries for justice echo into a void, unheard and unheeded, as biased laws tighten their grip, leaving him voiceless in a world that refuses to see his pain. When every door to salvation slams shut, he is left with no path but the one that leads to his own tragic end.

This book, The martyrs of legal terrorism, is a solemn tribute to these men—silent martyrs who, cornered by despair and forsaken by the very laws meant to protect them, found no solace, no reprieve. Each story is a heartrending testament to their unseen struggles, a plea for the world to acknowledge the agony of those who were failed by justice. They are the voiceless, whose whispers of anguish were drowned out by indifference and prejudice. Let these pages be their voice, a beacon to pierce the silence, demanding that their suffering be recognized and that no more lives be lost to the terror of a system that betrays its own.

This book is dedicated to all Innocent men who took their own lives under the weight of false accusations and relentless harassment—deserve more than silence. Their stories demand justice, not just for them, but for the countless others who continue to suffer in the shadows of this systemic exploitation.

This book is a tribute to their struggle and a plea for a more just and humane legal system.

RUDOLPH DSOUZA
25/04/2025

Introduction

In the grand halls of justice, where laws are meant to protect and uphold the dignity of all individuals, a silent crisis brews—one that remains largely ignored by society, the government, and even the very institutions sworn to ensure justice. This book, **The Martyrs of Legal Terrorism**, sheds light on a grave issue that has devastated countless lives: the rampant misuse of laws designed to protect women, which, instead, have become instruments of oppression against men.

In the corridors of justice, where the scales of fairness are meant to balance, a silent war rages—a war not fought with weapons, but with laws. This war has claimed countless lives, not in the battlefield, but within the sanctity of homes and courtrooms. It is a war waged by the misuse of legal provisions, a phenomenon the Supreme Court of India aptly termed "Legal Terrorism."

The term *Legal Terrorism* was coined by the Supreme Court of India to describe the growing trend of women misusing legal provisions to harass and torment their husbands and in-laws. Over the years, many innocent men, pushed to the brink of despair by false accusations and prolonged legal battles, have chosen death over a life of humiliation, injustice, and financial ruin. The handwritten notes of these men, found beside their lifeless bodies, narrate stories of betrayal, legal extortion, and societal neglect. Yet, their voices remain unheard, their sufferings dismissed, and their deaths unacknowledged by the system.

The term "Legal Terrorism" was coined to describe the systematic exploitation of laws designed to protect women, which are instead weaponized to harass, extort, and destroy husbands and their families. This is not merely about women misusing the law; it is a coordinated effort involving police, lawyers, family court judges, and even certain authorities who have turned the legal system into a blackmailing racket. The tools of this terror are well-known:

- Dowry Law (Section 498A)
- Domestic Violence Act
- Child Custody Battles
- Marital Rape Allegations
- POCSO (Protection of Children from Sexual Offences Act)
- Maintenance Claims

The misuse of laws like the Dowry Prohibition Act, the Protection of Women from Domestic Violence Act, Child Custody laws, Marital Rape allegations, the POCSO Act, and Maintenance laws has given rise to an unchecked wave of blackmail, corruption, and institutionalized harassment. What was originally intended as a safeguard for women has been weaponized to target men, creating a dangerous imbalance in the legal system. Corrupt police officials, manipulative lawyers, and biased family court judges often work in tandem to exploit legal loopholes, turning justice into an extortion racket.

These laws, intended to safeguard, have become instruments of oppression. Men, stripped of their dignity, are left with no recourse but to endure relentless harassment, financial ruin, and psychological trauma. For many, the torment becomes unbearable, leading them to the ultimate act of despair—suicide. Their final notes, scrawled in anguish, tell tales of a system that failed them, of a society that turned a blind eye, and of a legal machinery that became their executioner.

The bias against men in Indian society and its institutions is stark and undeniable. Despite clear evidence of increasing suicides among men due to legal harassment, the government refuses to acknowledge their plight. Official records by the National Crime Records Bureau (NCRB) do not even collect data on male victims, allowing the Women's Ministry to justify their inaction by claiming that no such issue exists. This deliberate oversight enables the continued victimization of men, who are forced to suffer in silence, with no legal recourse or societal support.

In a country where over 600 husbands are murdered by their wives every year, and thousands of men take their own lives after being falsely accused, it is time to break the silence. The statistics are chilling. In India, 600 murders of husbands by their wives have been recorded, yet these numbers barely scratch the surface. The National Crime Records Bureau (NCRB) lacks a separate section to document crimes against men, leaving their suffering unacknowledged by the state. The Ministry of Women and Child Development, in its silence, perpetuates the myth that men are not victims, even as the bodies pile up. *The Martyrs of Legal Terrorism* is not just a book; it is a movement to expose the dark side of a system that has failed its people. It is a call to recognize the suffering of men, to demand judicial reforms, and to put an end to the abuse of laws that were meant to protect, not persecute.

This book, *The Martyrs of Legal Terrorism*, is a testament to those who fell victim to this systemic bias. It is a call to action, urging society to recognize and address the plight of men who suffer in silence. It exposes the nexus of corruption within the legal system and challenges the government to enact gender-neutral laws that protect all citizens, regardless of gender.

The True-life stories within these pages are not just accounts of individual tragedies; they are indictments of a system that has lost its way. They are a plea for justice, for reform, and for the restoration of faith in the rule of law. Let the martyrs of legal terrorism not die in vain. Let their voices echo until the scales of justice are balanced once more.

The time has come to confront the truth: Legal Terrorism is not just a women's issue—it is a human issue. And it is one we can no longer afford to ignore.

Justice is not justice if it serves only one side. The battle against Legal Terrorism is not just about men's rights—it is about restoring balance, fairness, and integrity in the legal system. This book aims to be the voice for those who can no longer speak, for the men who suffered in silence, and for the families they left behind in the wake of their tragic deaths.

For decades, powerful lobbies have championed one-sided laws under the guise of empowering women, yet these laws have quietly claimed countless male lives, far outstripping other tragedies. Playing the victim has become a shield to justify wrongs, but the stark truth lies in the numbers. The National Crime Records Bureau (NCRB) statistics reveal a grim reality: men who did not die of natural causes but were driven to end their lives prematurely, broken by relentless torture and harassment enabled by biased laws and fuelled by certain women's organizations.

- The law must not favour one side.
- The law must not privilege one gender.
- The law must be blind.
- The law must be equal for all.

In memory of the martyrs lost to this legal terrorism and the men who perished in silent agony, Voice of the Voiceless amplifies their muted cries, resounding louder than the clamour of those who perpetuate injustice.

These men didn't just die; they left behind a legacy of suffering, of unheard cries, of lives destroyed by laws weaponized in the name of protection. Laws must not be for one gender. Laws must not be tools for revenge.

Justice must be blind—not blind to pain, but blind to prejudice. In memory of every man who died in silence, in honour of those who still live in fear, this book stands as an echo of that silence—a silence louder than the shouts of those who justify legal abuse.

This voice is a beacon of hope for future victims, and a call to those who carry forward the flame of their suffering and struggle against Legal Terrorism.

ARE YOU WITH ME?

How it started? And when.

India, a nation with a rich cultural heritage and a complex history, has long grappled with issues of gender inequality. While the country's legal framework has evolved significantly since independence in 1947, the introduction of laws perceived as favoring women has sparked debate about their necessity, impact, and fairness. These laws, often enacted to address systemic discrimination and violence against women, emerged primarily in the post-independence era, with significant momentum from the 1960s onward. Their roots lie in a combination of historical patriarchal practices, social reform movements, and modern feminist advocacy, but their perceived one-sidedness has raised concerns about unintended consequences, including the marginalization of men. This essay explores when these laws began, why they were introduced, and the broader context that shaped their development, while critically examining their implications.

Historical Context and the Emergence of Women-Centric Laws

The status of women in India has been shaped by centuries of patriarchal traditions, where practices like sati, child marriage, and dowry reinforced gender hierarchies. During the Vedic period, women enjoyed relative equality, but by the medieval era, their rights were curtailed, as reflected in texts like Tulsidas's couplet equating women with those deserving punishment. Colonial rule under the British (1757–1947) introduced some reforms, such as the Bengal Sati Regulation (1829) and the Hindu Widows' Remarriage Act (1856), driven by Indian reformers like Raja Ram Mohan Roy and British administrators. However, these were limited and did not address systemic gender disparities.

The post-independence period marked a turning point. The Constitution of India (1950) enshrined equality under Article 14 and empowered the state to make special provisions for women and children under Article 15(3). This constitutional mandate laid the groundwork for women-centric legislation, driven by the recognition that women faced unique disadvantages due to patriarchal norms. The Dowry Prohibition Act of 1961 was one of the earliest post-independence laws aimed at protecting women from dowry-related harassment and violence, a practice that often led to abuse or death. However, its enforcement was weak, and dowry-related issues persisted, highlighting the need for stronger measures.

The 1970s and 1980s saw a surge in women-centric laws, spurred by feminist activism and high-profile cases of violence against women. The Mathura rape case (1972), where the Supreme Court acquitted the accused citing the victim's "loose moral character," triggered nationwide protests and led to the Criminal

Law Amendment Act of 1983. This law strengthened protections against sexual violence, shifted the burden of proof to perpetrators in custodial rape cases, and prohibited revealing victims' identities. Similarly, the Shah Bano case (1985), where the Supreme Court granted maintenance to a divorced Muslim woman, highlighted the vulnerability of women post-divorce. Although the subsequent Muslim Women (Protection of Rights on Divorce) Act of 1986 limited maintenance rights due to political pressures, it underscored the push for legal protections for women.

The 2000s marked a further intensification of women-centric legislation. The Protection of Women from Domestic Violence Act (2005) provided comprehensive safeguards against physical, emotional, and economic abuse, empowering women to seek protection orders and maintenance. The Sexual Harassment of Women at Workplace (Prevention, Prohibition and Redressal) Act (2013), catalyzed by the Vishaka Guidelines (1997) following the Bhanwari Devi case, addressed workplace harassment. The Criminal Law (Amendment) Act of 2013, enacted after the 2012 Delhi gang rape, expanded definitions of sexual violence, criminalized stalking and voyeurism, and imposed stricter penalties. These laws were designed to address the alarming prevalence of violence against women, with statistics indicating that 79% of Indian girls face physical violence and dowry deaths occur every seven minutes.

Reasons Behind Women-Centric Laws

The enactment of these laws was driven by several interconnected factors:

Historical Gender Disparities: India's patriarchal history marginalized women, denying them property rights, education, and autonomy. Practices like female infanticide, child marriage, and dowry underscored their vulnerability. The Hindu Succession Act of 1956, for instance, initially excluded women from inheriting ancestral property, a gap partially addressed by the 2005 amendment granting daughters equal rights. Laws favoring women were seen as corrective measures to counter centuries of systemic oppression.

Social Reform and Feminist Movements: The women's suffrage movement in the early 20th century and post-independence feminist activism played crucial roles. Organizations like the Women's Indian Association and protests following cases like Mathura and Bhanwari Devi pressured the government to act. The second wave of feminism, though slower to reach India, amplified demands for legal protections against violence and discrimination.

High Incidence of Violence Against Women: Statistics underscored the urgency of legal intervention. The National Crime Records Bureau (NCRB) reported rising cases of dowry deaths, domestic violence, and sexual assault. The 2012 Delhi gang rape case, which sparked nationwide protests, highlighted the need for robust laws to ensure women's safety. Laws like the 2013 Criminal Law Amendment were direct responses to public outrage and the government's pledge of "zero tolerance" for violence against women.

Constitutional Mandate and International Influence: Article 15(3) of the Constitution explicitly allows special provisions for women, reflecting the state's commitment to gender justice. International frameworks, such as the UN Charter and conventions on women's rights, also influenced India's legal reforms. The global rise of feminism and India's emergence as a modernizing economy further necessitated laws to enhance women's socioeconomic participation, as gender disparities were seen as detrimental to national progress.

Political Expediency: In some cases, laws were enacted as reactive measures to appease public sentiment or political constituencies. The 2013 legislation following the Delhi gang rape, for instance, was criticized as a "knee-jerk" response, with analysts noting that laws alone cannot change deep-rooted cultural attitudes. Similarly, the Shah Bano case saw political maneuvering that diluted women's rights to maintenance, reflecting the complex interplay of religion, politics, and gender.

Critical Examination: One-Sidedness and Its Implications

While these laws were introduced with the bona fide intention of protecting women, critics argue they have become one-sided, sometimes leading to misuse and injustice against men. The Domestic Violence Act (2005), for example, does not allow men to file complaints, leaving male victims of abuse without legal recourse. Section 498A of the Indian Penal Code, which addresses cruelty by husbands and in-laws, has been criticized for its stringent non-bailable provisions, with reports of false cases being filed to settle personal scores. The NCRB data, while highlighting female victims, also reveals a significant number of male suicides linked to domestic disputes and legal harassment, suggesting that men are not immune to victimization.

Law made by crying Victim.

Feminist movements, particularly from the 1970s onward, amplified these issues through protests and advocacy. High-profile cases, such as the Mathura rape case (1972), where the Supreme Court's acquittal of the accused sparked outrage, and the 2012 Delhi gang rape, which led to the Criminal Law (Amendment) Act of 2013, galvanized public and political support for stronger laws. These incidents framed women as victims of systemic violence, creating moral and social pressure for legislative action. Advocacy by women's organizations, such as

the All India Democratic Women's Association,
emphasized victimhood to highlight the urgency of
reform, often citing data like the 79% of Indian girls
facing physical violence or the occurrence of a dowry
death every seven minutes.

Laws are often amended or strengthened with
harsher punishments based on one or two high-
profile incidents, overlooking the grim reality of 600
men murdered annually by their wives and the
staggering rate of male suicides—three times higher
than female suicides, with one man ending his life
every 4.5 minutes compared to one woman every
seven minutes. Yet, feminist lobbies, by emphasizing
women's victimhood, have obscured these findings,
resisting efforts to enact gender-neutral laws or laws
protecting men. Such reforms would enable the
NCRB to collect comprehensive data on male victims,
challenging the narrative of perpetual female
victimhood in a data-driven world and complicating
the ability of women's organizations to consistently
claim victim status.

The perception of one-sidedness stems from several
factors. First, the laws are gender-specific, focusing
exclusively on women as victims, which overlooks
male vulnerabilities. Second, weak enforcement
mechanisms and societal biases often lead to
misuse, as women may exploit legal provisions to
harass men, particularly in dowry or divorce cases.
Third, the judiciary's tendency to tilt toward women

in gender-related cases, as noted in cases like *Dr. N.G. Dastane v. S. Dastane*, can undermine fairness. Critics argue that this approach risks replacing one form of inequality with another, where men face legal terrorism—systemic harassment through biased laws.

However, defenders of these laws argue that they are necessary given the scale of violence against women and the persistent gender gap. With only 23% of women in India's labor force compared to 72.7% of men, and women having 74.4% of the economic rights of men, the structural disadvantages women face justify affirmative legal measures. The high prevalence of dowry deaths, sexual harassment, and domestic violence further underscores the need for protective laws. Moreover, cultural norms that prioritize male heirs and perpetuate practices like sex-selective abortions necessitate a legal framework that empowers women.

The "crying victim" critique suggests that women, through feminist groups or individual cases, have exaggerated or manipulated their victimhood to gain legal advantages. This perspective points to several mechanisms:

Public Sympathy and Media Amplification: High-profile cases of violence against women often receive extensive media coverage, shaping public perception. For instance, the 2012 Delhi gang rape case dominated headlines, with protests framing women as universally vulnerable. This emotional appeal pressured lawmakers to act swiftly, resulting in laws like the 2013 amendment, which expanded definitions of sexual violence and imposed harsher penalties. Critics argue that such cases, while tragic, are used to generalize women's victimhood, overshadowing male victims or nuanced discussions.

Feminist Advocacy and Lobbying: Women's organizations have been instrumental in drafting and pushing for laws like the Protection of Women from Domestic Violence Act (2005) and the Sexual Harassment of Women at Workplace Act (2013). By presenting women as a uniformly oppressed group, these groups have secured provisions that are gender-specific, such as maintenance rights or protection orders exclusive to women. Critics contend that this framing ignores male victims of abuse, as seen in the lack of provisions for men under the 2005 Act.

Legal and Political Expediency: Politicians often respond to public outcry to gain favor or defuse crises. The Shah Bano case (1985), where a divorced Muslim woman's maintenance claim led to a Supreme Court ruling, illustrates how women's victimhood can become a political tool. Although the subsequent 1986 Act limited maintenance rights due to religious backlash, the case highlighted how women's plight can be leveraged to push legal changes. Critics argue that such reactive law making prioritizes optics over fairness, leading to laws like Section 498A of the Indian Penal Code, which addresses cruelty by husbands but is criticized for misuse due to its non-bailable nature.

Cultural Narratives: Indian society often views women as inherently vulnerable, Victim, Abla naari; a stereotype that feminist advocacy sometimes reinforces to secure protections. This narrative can lead to laws that assume women's victimhood, such as automatic arrests under dowry harassment cases, even when evidence is lacking. The Supreme Court in *Arnesh Kumar v. State of Bihar* (2014) noted the misuse of Section 498A, suggesting that some women exploit these laws to settle personal scores, lending credence to the "crying victim" critique.

Evidence and Criticisms

The "crying victim" narrative gains traction due to documented instances of legal misuse. NCRB data from 2019–2021 shows a significant number of acquittals in dowry and domestic violence cases, with some estimates suggesting 10–15% of Section 498A cases may be false or exaggerated. Men's rights groups, active on platforms like X, cite cases where men face harassment through frivolous lawsuits, leading to financial ruin, social stigma, and, in extreme cases, suicide. NCRB data also indicates that men account for over 70% of suicides in India, with domestic disputes and legal pressures often cited as factors. These statistics fuel arguments that women-centric laws, by assuming male guilt, create a form of "legal terrorism."

Conclusion: Toward a Balanced Legal Framework

The journey of women-centric laws in India began in earnest post-independence, with significant milestones in the 1960s, 1980s, and 2000s, driven by the need to address historical injustices, respond to violence, and align with constitutional and international commitments. These laws were necessitated by a patriarchal society that marginalized women, but their gender-specific nature has sparked concerns about fairness and misuse. While they have undoubtedly empowered women and raised awareness, the rising number of male suicides and reports of legal harassment suggest that the pendulum may have swung too far in some cases.

This imbalance has led to legal asymmetry—where the rights of men in certain legal scenarios are not equally protected. Over time, many families, including elderly parents, have been implicated in false cases. The National Crime Records Bureau (NCRB) has reported rising cases of male suicides, particularly among married men, many of whom cite family or legal harassment as a cause—yet there remains no dedicated mechanism to address men's grievances in such matters.

Achieving true gender equality requires a balanced legal framework that protects all individuals, regardless of gender. Laws should be gender-neutral where possible, addressing abuse and injustice without assuming victimhood based on sex. Strengthening enforcement, raising legal literacy, and fostering cultural change are critical to ensuring that laws serve their intended purpose without creating new victims. As India strives for inclusivity, the challenge lies in crafting a system where justice is blind, echoing the constitutional promise of equality for all

Bias

Bias, in simple terms, refers to an unfair inclination toward one group over another. When applied to the judicial system, bias manifests in various forms-favouritism in verdicts, preferential treatment of certain individuals, or even an outright disregard for fairness. This bias is not just limited to class or religion but extends deeply into gender-based discrimination, where men often find themselves at the receiving end of systemic injustice.

The judicial system, which is expected to be the epitome of fairness, frequently displays gender bias in numerous ways. Judges may favour one party over another due to personal relationships, preconceived notions, or societal pressures. In some cases, legal proceedings become skewed, with certain attorneys receiving preferential treatment, or cases being assigned to judges based on hidden agendas rather than merit. A fundamental principle of justice is that no judge should preside over a case in which they have a vested interest; however, biases-both conscious and unconscious-continue to erode this ideal.

Systemic Bias:

Presumption of Guilt: The legal system often presumes the husband's guilt, requiring men to prove their innocence rather than the accuser to prove the allegations. This imbalance encourages misuse.

No Penalties for False Cases: The lack of stringent penalties for filing false complaints acts as a deterrent against misuse, emboldening women to exploit the law.

Impact on Families

Extended Families Targeted: Women often include in-laws in DV complaints, dragging entire families into legal battles. This tactic is used to pressure men into compliance.

Child Custody Battles: False DV allegations are frequently used to gain an upper hand in custody disputes, leveraging the court's bias in favour of the mother.

While the PWDVA was designed to protect women, its one-sided nature and lack of safeguards against misuse have turned it into a weapon of legal terrorism against men. The absence of gender-neutral provisions and penalties for false complaints exacerbates the problem, leaving men vulnerable to exploitation and harassment. Addressing this imbalance is crucial to ensuring justice for all.

Social Bias:

Assumption of Male Perpetrators: Society stereotypes men as perpetrators, dismissing their vulnerabilities. Issues like domestic abuse against men or exploitation, harassments, crimes by wives are rarely acknowledged.

Mental Health Neglect: Men's mental health struggles are often ignored, leading to alarming suicide rates. Married men are three times more likely to die by suicide than married women, yet their struggles remain underreported.

Lack of Support Systems: Organizations advocating for men's rights, such as Purush Ayog, highlight the absence of resources and societal support for men facing abuse or harassment.

Institutional Bias:

Lack of Legal Protections: Unlike women, men have no specific legal provisions to protect them from harassment or exploitation, leaving them exposed to misuse of laws.

NCRB Data Gap: The NCRB does not categorize crimes against men separately, masking the scale of their suffering and allowing the narrative of male privilege to persist.

Reverse Sexism in Workplaces: Studies indicate that discrimination against men in female-dominated workplaces is more prevalent than discrimination against women in male-dominated sectors, yet this remains unaddressed.

Cultural Bias:

Son Preference: While sons are traditionally preferred for economic reasons, this preference does not translate into societal empathy for their struggles. Instead, men are expected to be stoic providers, with their emotional and psychological needs ignored.

Double Standards in Relationships: Men are often held to higher standards of behaviour, while women's actions in marital or familial disputes are rarely scrutinized with the same rigor.

Legal Bias:

Dowry Laws (Section 498A): While designed to protect women, these laws are frequently misused to harass husbands and their families. The legal presumption of guilt on men, without evidence, underscores a significant imbalance.

Child Custody: Under the Hindu Minority and Guardianship Act, 1956, mothers are often granted custody of children below five years, side-lining fathers' rights to maintain meaningful relationships with their children and women also use child to get maintenance from father.

Marital Rape and POCSO: Allegations of marital rape or sexual offenses under POCSO are increasingly used as tools of extortion, with men often presumed guilty until proven innocent. Women are using Girl child against Father with false POCSO so to deny visitation or Custody

Maintenance Laws: Men are disproportionately burdened with financial responsibilities, even in cases of false allegations or mutual separation, leaving them financially crippled.

The Protection of Women from Domestic Violence Act (PWDVA), 2005, was enacted to safeguard women from abuse in domestic relationships. However, over the years, there have been growing concerns about its misuse as a tool to harass and extort men. Here's how women exploit this one-sided law:

Gender Bias in Courts:

When discussing gender bias, many assume it to be neutral, affecting both men and women in different situations. However, in reality, legal bias overwhelmingly favours women in multiple aspects. Courts have historically leaned towards women in cases related to domestic disputes, divorce settlements, and child custody, often disregarding the legitimate concerns of men.

Andrea Miller, a renowned expert on judicial behaviour, stated: "Many judges are not able to factor out their personal beliefs while they are considering court cases, even when they have the best possible intentions." This highlights the tendency of judges to make decisions influenced by their own experiences and prejudices, which significantly impacts male litigants.

One of the most glaring examples of gender bias in the judicial system is the allocation of child custody. Even when both parents have equal qualifications, work profiles, and financial stability, the courts disproportionately award custody to mothers. This stems from the outdated belief that a child is better off with the mother rather than the father, despite growing evidence that children thrive with both parental figures actively involved in their upbringing. Such judicial decisions reinforce a systemic bias that disregards the role of fathers in their children's lives.

Moreover, the selection and appointment of judges also reflect gender bias. In some instances, personal hardships faced by judges in their own lives influence their judgments, leading them to sympathize with a particular gender. This personal bias seeps into verdicts, ultimately impacting the fairness of legal proceedings.

The consequences of this systemic bias are far-reaching. Men falsely accused of crimes such as domestic violence, dowry harassment, or sexual assault endure emotional distress, social stigma, and financial ruin. Many end up losing their jobs, families, and reputations, while the legal system continues to operate with little accountability for false accusations. The unchecked misuse of protective laws by certain individuals, combined with a judiciary that often presumes men to be the perpetrators, has turned legal justice into an instrument of gender-based discrimination.

The judiciary, along with law enforcement agencies and government bodies, must acknowledge and address this growing disparity. Laws designed to protect women must not be misused as tools of oppression against men. A truly just system should ensure fairness for all, rather than favouring one gender at the expense of another.

The fight for justice is not about denying protection to one group but about ensuring that fairness and equality are upheld for everyone, regardless of gender. The time has come for society, the government, and the judiciary to recognize the silent suffering of men and take corrective measures to restore balance in the legal system.

Indian society, deeply rooted in patriarchal norms earlier, has long been associated with gender inequality against women. However, beneath this surface lies a less-discussed but equally pressing issue: systemic bias against boys and men. This bias manifests in legal, social, and institutional frameworks, often rendering men vulnerable to exploitation and neglect.

False Allegations

Weaponizing DV Complaints: Women often file domestic violence (DV) cases to settle personal scores, exact revenge, or gain leverage in marital disputes. These complaints are sometimes baseless, aimed at pressuring men into financial settlements or custody agreements.

Exaggerated Claims: Some women exaggerate or fabricate incidents of abuse to strengthen their case, knowing that the law prioritizes their testimony over evidence.

Financial Exploitation

Maintenance Demands: The PWDVA allows women to claim maintenance, residence, and monetary relief. Many misuse this provision to demand exorbitant sums, even in cases of mutual separation or false allegations.

Residence Rights: Women can claim the right to reside in the marital home, often forcing men and their families out of their own property, even without proof of abuse.

Legal Harassment

Non-Bailable Offenses: Domestic violence cases under Section 498A of the Indian Penal Code (IPC) are non-bailable, leading to immediate arrest of the accused husband and his family members, even before investigation. This provision is exploited to inflict severe legal and emotional distress.

Long Legal Battles: The process of proving innocence in DV cases is lengthy and costly, draining men financially and emotionally. Even if acquitted, the stigma and legal trauma remain.

Psychological and Social Impact

Public Shaming: False DV complaints tarnish men's reputations, affecting their personal, professional, and social lives. The mere accusation can lead to ostracization and mental trauma.

Family Pressure: Men often face pressure to settle cases out of court to avoid societal stigma or prolonged legal battles, even when they are innocent.

Indian society, while often perceived as patriarchal, has deep-seated biases that also work against men in various ways. Here's how:

Expectation to be Providers: Men are expected to be the breadwinners, carrying the financial burden of the entire family. There is little societal sympathy for men who struggle financially or face unemployment.

Lack of Emotional Support: From childhood, boys are conditioned to suppress emotions and are discouraged from expressing vulnerability, as it is seen as a sign of weakness. Society offers minimal mental health support for men, leading to high suicide rates.

Discriminatory Legal Framework: Laws such as the Dowry Act, Domestic Violence Act, and Maintenance laws disproportionately favour women. Even if men are falsely accused, they face lengthy trials, financial losses, and social stigma.

Father's Rights in Child Custody: In cases of divorce, courts overwhelmingly grant custody to mothers, often disregarding the role of fathers in parenting. Even when fathers are financially and emotionally capable, they are reduced to mere visitors in their children's lives.

Unrecognized Domestic Abuse Against Men: While laws exist to protect women from domestic violence, there are no legal provisions for men who face abuse from their spouses. Cases of verbal, emotional, and physical abuse against men are often ignored or ridiculed.

Workplace Discrimination: Gender diversity policies and quotas often favour women, leading to instances where men may be overlooked for promotions or jobs, despite equal qualifications and better performance.

No Legal Protection Against Sexual Harassment: Workplace harassment laws focus on women, leaving men with no legal recourse if they are harassed by female colleagues or superiors. False allegations can destroy a man's career and reputation.

Neglect of Male Suicides: The suicide rate among men in India is significantly higher than that of women, often due to financial stress, false accusations, or domestic conflicts. However, there is little recognition or support for male mental health.

Military and Risky Jobs: Men are expected to take up dangerous professions, including the army, police, and firefighting, with little regard for their well-being or the risks involved. Their sacrifices are often taken for granted.

Social and Cultural Expectations: From paying for dates to handling all wedding expenses, men are expected to prove their worth through financial means, reinforcing an unfair burden on them.

The Bias by Birth

Discrimination against men remains a largely unexamined and underreported issue, with no comprehensive research data or studies on their mental health documented in existing scientific literature. Such bias and discrimination profoundly impact men's lives-physically, mentally, emotionally, and psychologically-and constitute a fundamental violation of human rights. Tragically, most instances of discrimination against men go unreported, unnoticed, or ignored, often leading to denial of acceptance by families, divorce, depression, or even suicide in extreme cases.

Many men who are abused or discriminated against face victimization from an early age or during childhood. However, societal expectations of masculinity often compel men to suffer in silence, as they perceive no alternative. The abuse and discrimination they endure frequently stem from their own communities or families, further complicating their ability to seek help.

Men are also more hesitant than women to disclose their victimization, fearing ridicule, shame, and societal judgment. Many have never even confided in close family members about their struggles. The pervasive societal view of "proper masculine behaviour" discourages men from expressing or confronting discrimination, making them even more vulnerable. The lack of support systems and resources has ensured that the most severe forms of discrimination against men remain hidden to this day.

The long-term negative effects of such discrimination are particularly pronounced in men who are the primary breadwinners for their families. Contrary to the misconception that abused men do not suffer psychologically, empirical evidence reveals no significant gender differences in psychosomatic illness or stress levels. Discrimination forces men to live in a state of chronic depression, often leading to premature death.

Globally, research on the repercussions of discrimination on men's health remains a non-priority, overshadowing the reality that men are equally vulnerable to its devastating effects. Socioeconomic factors, societal influences, and the consistent failure of governments to provide support exacerbate this issue. However, these challenges can be addressed by ensuring that men receive the necessary help, resources, and support to improve their quality of life and overcome the systemic biases they face.

Society vs. Men: The Unseen Struggles

No man is born a criminal-his environment, circumstances, and societal pressures shape his actions. Society, which includes family, economic conditions, and social norms, plays a crucial role in a man's upbringing. A supportive family, quality education, and a healthy social environment foster responsible individuals. However, when a system is biased against men, it can push many toward frustration, helplessness, or even crime.

Despite their hardships, men receive little to no support from society. Masculinity is often equated with endurance and sacrifice, leading to the widespread belief that only women suffer and that men must bear all burdens without complaint. This bias is deeply ingrained, as society perceives women as the weaker sex, deserving of sympathy and protection, while men are expected to be providers, protectors, and problem-solvers-without room for vulnerability.

In the modern digital age, the media further amplifies this disparity. Television, the internet, and print media glorify women's struggles while ignoring men's hardships. Any content that portrays male suffering is either trivialized or dismissed. Women receive overwhelming support from legal frameworks, government policies, NGOs, and feminist organizations, while men are largely left to fend for themselves.

This study, conducted in India, highlights the silent suffering of Indian men. According to research by *MyNation Hope Foundation* (NGO), despite the absence of government support for men, the majority continue to struggle with dignity. They work long hours, travel to distant cities for employment, and endure harsh conditions just to provide for their families.

95% of financial support for families comes from men, while only 5% of women contribute significantly.

Men often commute long distances and survive on a single meal per day just to ensure their families have enough to eat.

Society expects men to pay all household expenses, while women are generally excused from financial responsibilities.

The gendered expectation that a man must be the sole provider creates immense financial, emotional, and psychological pressure, yet there are no policies or welfare schemes to assist struggling men.

Women vs. Men: Legal Bias and Systemic Injustice

India's criminal laws, including the IPC and CrPC, are heavily biased in favour of women. Many special laws enacted for the welfare of women have been crafted under feminist influence, often without considering their misuse. These laws are frequently drafted in a vague and broad manner, leaving them open to misinterpretation and exploitation by disgruntled or vindictive individuals.

The Role of Feminist Lobbying in Legal Misuse

Feminist groups, often referred to as the "feminist mafia," aggressively lobby for laws that benefit only Some women. These laws are pushed through without check of misuse or scrutiny. Once implemented, they become tools for harassment, financial extortion, and even legal terrorism against men.

They lack clarity and seem designed not to serve justice but to increase litigation, benefiting lawyers, police, and legal professionals.

Governments hesitate to challenge these one-sided laws, fearing backlash from the female voter base, which constitutes nearly 50% of the population.

Dismissing men's suffering has become a political strategy, ensuring continuous funding for women-centric organizations, even when studies prove that women are equally capable of committing domestic violence, abuse, and crime.

Challenging the Myth of Women as "Only Victims"

There is strong empirical evidence that women are not always the victims in cases of domestic abuse or interpersonal violence. However, this contradicts the feminist narrative, which thrives on portraying women as helpless victims to justify continuous government funding.

Governments and feminist groups ignore research showing that women can be equally violent in relationships.

Funding is directed exclusively toward women's welfare, while men's issues are completely neglected.

Organizations such as the National Commission for Women (NCW) have failed to address domestic violence in a gender-neutral manner.

Crime and Gender Bias in the Legal System

Indian laws empower women to commit crimes with impunity. In numerous cases, women have been found abetting, instigating, or even directly committing crimes, yet they escape severe punishment due to gender-biased laws.

A woman who abets a man's suicide rarely faces more than 2-3 years of punishment, while a man convicted of similar offenses receives a life sentence.

Women can file false cases of dowry harassment, domestic violence, or rape, and even if proven false, they face no punishment.

Studies indicate that women have played direct or indirect roles in many crimes, yet their accountability is almost never questioned.

State-Sponsored Bias

According to a study conducted by MyNation Hope Foundation (NGO) focusing exclusively on Indian men, there are no government-provided support schemes specifically designed to address the unique challenges faced by men in India. While the Government of India has introduced numerous initiatives for women, these programs highlight a glaring gender bias, leaving men without any dedicated support systems. Below is a list of various government schemes exclusively aimed at women, which starkly contrasts the complete absence of similar efforts for men:

Government of India Schemes ONLY for Women

- Mother and Child Tracking System (MCTS)
- Pradhan Mantri Matritva Vandana Yojana
- Rajiv Gandhi Scheme for Empowerment of Adolescent Girls
- Sabla Rashtriya Mahila Kosh
- National Action Plan for Children
- Digital Laado(Girl Child Education and Empowerment)
- Beti Bachao Beti Padhao Scheme
- One Stop Centre Scheme
- Emergency Response and Rescue Services
- Medical Assistance
- Assistance in lodging FIR/NCR/DIR

- Psycho-social support and counselling
- Legal aid and counselling
- Shelter
- Video Conferencing Facility for police/courts
- Women Helpline Scheme (24 Hours)
- UJJAWALA: A Comprehensive Scheme for Prevention of Trafficking and Rehabilitation of Victims
- Working Women Hostel
- SWADHAR Greh(A Scheme for Women in Difficult Circumstances)
- Support to Training and Employment Programme for Women (STEP)
- Nari Shakti Puraskar, Stree Shakti Puruskar, Nari Shakti Puruskar, Rajya Mahila Samman, Zila Mahila Samman
- Mahila Police Volunteers
- Mahila E-Haat
- Mahila Shakti Kendras (MSK)
- NIRBHAYA

State-Specific Schemes for Women

Goa:

- Kanyadhan Scheme: Financial assistance of Rs.25,000 for daughters' marriages.
- Mamta Scheme: Rs.5,000 incentive for mothers delivering a female child.
- Dhanalaxmi Scheme: Rs.25,000 fixed deposit for newborn girls.

- Yashaswini Scheme: Rs.1 lakh financial assistance to self-help groups.
- Shelter Home for Women: Temporary shelter and skill training.
- Grih Adhar Scheme: Rs.1,000 monthly assistance to housewives from low-income families.

Haryana:

- Swayamsidha,
- Swa-Shakti,
- Balika Samridhi,
- Hostel for working women,
- Swadhar,
- Kishori Shakti Yojana,
- Ladli.

West Bengal:

- Kanyashree Prakalpa: Annual scholarship of Rs.750 and a one-time grant of Rs.25,000 for girls aged 13-19.

Maharashtra:

- Mazi Kanya Bhagyashree Scheme: Financial aid of Rs.5,000 for the first five years, followed by Rs.2,500-Rs.3,000 annually, and Rs.1 lakh for education after age 18.

Karnataka:

Bhagyashree Scheme: Health insurance cover up to Rs.25,000 and scholarships.

Madhya Pradesh:

- Ladli Laxmi Yojana: National Saving Certificates worth Rs.6,000 annually for five years.
- Perks Beyond Government Schemes
- Free bicycles for girls
- Education seat reservations
- Transport seat reservations
- Ladies-only buses and trains
- Women-only queues
- Free bus rides in Delhi
- Free legal assistance and PIL support

The Hypocrisy of Gender Politics

While feminists frequently criticize patriarchy, men are burdened by the very same system they are accused of perpetuating. Men are often expected to be the sole providers for their families, sometimes spanning multiple generations, yet they receive no support from the government or society. This unjust burden can drive men to commit crimes out of desperation. However, unlike women, who are often excused for crimes due to reasons like "depression" or "abuse," men are rarely afforded such leniency.

The deeply ingrained perception of women as the "weaker sex" also results in harsher penalties for men committing the same crimes, exposing them to longer sentences and a higher likelihood of turning into repeat offenders.

The Financial Divide

The Women's Ministry receives over Rs.100,000 crore in grants annually, yet there is little evidence that even 10% of this is utilized for women's empowerment. Some theories suggest that a significant portion of these funds may be diverted for political use, Cut to Ministers and Politicians.

The Core Question

When 95% of taxpayers are men, and 95% of men work tirelessly, often sacrificing their health and lives to support their families, why is there not a single scheme or plan to support men in India? This blatant disparity not only exposes systemic gender bias but also perpetuates the very inequality it claims to fight against.

Legal System vs. Men

The Government of India has enacted numerous one-sided and biased laws that overwhelmingly favour women while leaving men without any dedicated legal protections or support schemes. This systemic imbalance has created a judicial environment where men face severe social, economic, cultural, and political disadvantages, permeating every aspect of their lives.

Unconscious Bias in the Justice System

Men's experiences within the legal system, from their initial interactions with the police to their courtroom battles, reveal a pervasive unconscious bias against them. The unholy nexus between feminist groups, law enforcement, and lawyers often results in unjust practices, which the government has yet to address.

For example, the use of legal terminology and the limited legal options available to men create significant barriers to justice. Even when men are acquitted or granted bail, the collateral consequences of conviction-such as lifelong stigma and discrimination-persist. Once labelled a criminal, a man is often ostracized and excluded from society, regardless of his actual guilt.

Judicial Hypocrisy and Bias

Judicial decisions often reflect a conscious or unconscious bias against men. In one case, the Supreme Court acquitted a woman who murdered her husband, citing "sudden and grave provocation" after he called her a prostitute (*Nawaz vs. The State Rep. by Inspector of Police*). However, it is unlikely that the court would extend the same leniency to a man in a similar situation.

In another instance, the Gujarat High Court ruled that a one-night stand does not constitute adultery (*Sharmilaben vs. Pravinsinh Balvantsinh Solanki*). Such rulings underscore the unequal treatment of men and women within the justice system.

Misuse of Laws and Feminist Agenda

Scientific evidence confirms that women are no less violent than men. Yet, feminist groups have systematically silenced researchers, media, and law enforcement agencies to suppress evidence of female-perpetrated violence and false allegations of abuse or harassment.

For example, when a judge referred to Section 498A of the IPC as a tool of legal terrorism, women's groups protested violently, damaging public property and disrupting court proceedings. This blatant intimidation highlights the double standards embedded in the legal system.

Crime Prevention and Systemic Neglect

The National Crime Records Bureau (NCRB) identifies unemployment, poverty, and low per capita income as contributing factors to crime. However, the government has failed to address these issues by providing education, training, or employment opportunities for men.

Instead, policies overwhelmingly favour women, leading to economic exclusion for men. Acts like the Maternity Benefit Act (1861), Protection of Women from Domestic Violence Act (2005), and Sexual Harassment of Women at Workplace Act (2013) are designed exclusively for women, leaving men vulnerable to exploitation and false allegations.

Lack of Legal Protections for Men

There are no laws to protect men from abuse, false allegations, or exploitation. The burden of proof in most cases lies entirely on men, despite the lack of evidence against them. This systemic neglect has led to a surge in male suicides, with men accounting for nearly double the number of suicides compared to women.

Economic Disparities and Gender Politics

While 95% of taxpayers are men, contributing to the nation's development, there are no schemes or policies to support their welfare. This blatant hypocrisy is evident in the absence of:

Recovery or rehabilitation centres for men

Acts to safeguard men's physical, economic, and family welfare

Data collection or research on crimes against men

Economic opportunities or training programs for men

The Urgent Need for Reform

The government's misandrist mindset and its embrace of feminist ideology have eroded the cultural, familial, and spiritual values that define India. By neglecting men's needs and perpetuating systemic bias, the state has driven countless men to despair, crime, and suicide.

It is imperative to enact gender-neutral laws, provide equal opportunities, and address the root causes of male vulnerability. Until then, the legal system will remain a tool of oppression against men, perpetuating inequality and injustice.

What Kills Men?

When family court turn slaughterhouses:

The characterization of Indian family courts as "slaughterhouses" or "Gestapos" for men arises from a perception-especially by those who harassed by Women centric laws or Legal Terrorism, that these family courts are heavily biased against men in matrimonial and family disputes. While these terms are hyperbolic and reflect frustration rather than an objective reality, they stem from systemic and procedural issues within the Indian family court system. Here's why this perception exists:

Perceived Gender Bias in Laws and Rulings

Indian family laws, such as Section 498A of the Indian Penal Code (anti-dowry law), the Domestic Violence Act, and maintenance provisions under Section 125 of the CrPC, are often criticized for favouring women. Critics argue that these laws assume male guilt and place the burden of proof on husbands, even in cases of false accusations. The Supreme Court itself has acknowledged that Section 498A is prone to misuse, with cases dragging on for years, financially and emotionally draining men.

Custody Disputes Favouring Mothers

In child custody cases, courts frequently award custody to mothers-especially for young children-based on the "tender years doctrine" or the assumption that women are naturally better caregivers. This often leaves fathers with limited access to their children, reinforcing the belief that the legal system is unfairly skewed, and these young children touted against father, when they grow up, they start to go against Father or refuse to meet him.

Maintenance and Alimony Rulings

Men are often ordered to pay significant amounts in maintenance or alimony, even in short-lived marriages or when they face financial hardship. The lack of a uniform formula for determining these payments, coupled with prolonged litigation, leads to perceptions of an exploitative system that unfairly burdens men.

Slow Judicial Process

Family court cases in India can take years to resolve due to overburdened courts and procedural delays. Critics argue that some women use these delays strategically to maximize financial settlements or exert emotional leverage-particularly in custody disputes. The prolonged nature of these cases is often seen as a punishment in itself.

Allegations of Extortion and Harassment

Some men claim that family courts enable legal extortion, where wives and their families file exaggerated or false claims-such as dowry harassment or domestic violence-to pressure men into settlements. The absence of strict penalties for false accusations exacerbates this grievance, making many men feel unprotected by the legal system. Women can file any number of Complaints/FIRs or cases as for her this is FREE of charge, In this case (Refer https://mynation.net/docs/316-2023/) Women file 45 FIRs but get 63 Lakhs Alimony too, for harassing Man, Still Indian Law support Women for misusing Law.

Cultural and Social Context

India's patriarchal past has led to laws aimed at protecting women from systemic abuse, but critics argue the system has now swung too far in the opposite direction, creating a "reverse bias." High-profile cases, such as that of Bengaluru techie Atul Subhash-who died by suicide in December 2024, allegedly due to harassment by his wife and in-laws-are cited as evidence of systemic failures against men. Some activists go as far as calling this a "state-sponsored male genocide". There are more men are committing suicide, It is men need special laws not the Women.

How maintenance is decided in India.

The primary criteria is simply being a woman-this is
the key factor Indian law considers. In the history of
India, not a single man has been awarded
maintenance, even in cases where the wife possesses
greater assets. Beyond this, the additional grounds for
maintenance are as follows:

Types of Maintenance in India

1.   Interim Maintenance (During Court
Proceedings)

- Under Section 125 CrPC, a wife (or dependent
  children/parents) can claim interim
  maintenance while the case is ongoing.

2.   Permanent Alimony (After Divorce)

- Courts decide whether maintenance should be
  a one-time lump sum or monthly payments.
- The lump sum is usually 1/3rd to 1/5th of
  the husband's net worth.

3.   Child Maintenance

- Child maintenance is separate from spousal
  maintenance and is granted based on the
  child's needs, education, and standard of
  living.

Legal Provisions for Alimony in India

1.   Hindus (Hindu Marriage Act, 1955 & Section 125 CrPC)

- Either spouse can claim alimony, but usually, the husband pays.

2.   Muslims (Muslim Personal Law & The Muslim Women (Protection of Rights on Divorce) Act, 1986)

- A Muslim woman can claim Mehr (dower) and Iddat (post-divorce support for 3 months).
- If she cannot support herself after Iddat, she can claim maintenance under Section 125 CrPC.

3.   Christians (Indian Divorce Act, 1869)

- The wife can claim maintenance up to 1/5th of the husband's income.

4.   Parsis (Parsi Marriage and Divorce Act, 1936)

- The wife can claim maintenance based on the husband's ability to pay.

5.   Special Marriage Act, 1954 (For Interfaith Marriages)

- Similar provisions to the Hindu Marriage Act.

6.   Domestic Violence Act, 2005

- A wife in a live-in relationship can claim maintenance under this law.

Legal Extortion:

Indian courts consider multiple factors to ensure fairness and financial stability for the dependent spouse, typically the wife. For Indian Women claiming Alimony/Maintenance is a Birth right. Once maintenance is granted, it is often treated as a permanent obligation, regardless of the husband's financial condition, age, or employment status. Courts have even ruled that a man must find a way to pay-whether by begging, borrowing, stealing, selling assets, or in extreme cases, even suggesting selling organs.

Key aspects such as the duration of the marriage, the wife's contributions, or her support to the husband are often overlooked. Women can claim maintenance even after a mutual consent divorce and may seek multiple revisions for enhancement at any time. The husband's pre-marriage assets and any financial growth post-divorce-achieved through his own efforts-can still be subject to claims, even if the wife remains unemployed to claim maintenance. Courts frequently grant such claims without significant scrutiny.

All Above laws only talk about granting Maintenance to Women, nothing for Men.

Women left her own, Man has to Pay

Women run away with Lover, Man has to Pay

Women harass, file dozens of False cases, Man has to Pay

Women kill husband, with the help of lover, still she get all husbands assets.

Man catch women in Adultery, still Man has to pay.

Marriage is one day old, Still Man has to pay.

No matter what, Man has to Pay, **BEG BORROW OR STEAL, BUT PAY**, anyone can search for these words to find where judges Boldly say.

In most parts of the world, during maintenance cases, only the assets jointly created by both partners during the course of the marriage are considered. Contributions and sacrifices made by both parties are taken into account, Assets acquired before the marriage or after the divorce are generally excluded. However, in India, during maintenance proceedings, the man's current assets are assessed at the time of the application, regardless of when they were acquired. A woman can file for maintenance at any time, claiming a change in circumstances—even if she is not working, living leisurely, or in a relationship with someone else— while the man is struggling to rebuild his life post-divorce.

There are no clear time limits on maintenance, and the duration of the marriage often isn't considered. A woman can also take custody of the children and file for maintenance again in the children's names. In some cases, even for a father to visit his child, courts require large financial deposits. For example, in the author's own case, the High Court of Karnataka ordered him to deposit ?10 lakhs (1 million rupees) just for a single child visit, along with surrendering his passport to the police. This illustrates the biased nature of the judiciary—it not only drains men financially but also treats them like criminals.

A More Balanced Perspective

Despite these grievances, the "slaughterhouse" label remains a subjective and emotive overstatement. Family courts were established under the Family Courts Act of 1984 to promote conciliation and speedy resolution of disputes, not to discriminate against any gender. Women, too, face significant challenges, such as delays in receiving maintenance or social stigma in divorce proceedings. While the Supreme Court has acknowledged the misuse of certain laws like Section 498A and suggested reforms (It was a just eyewash), systemic change has been slow. In reality, family courts often function as recovery agents for women. In maintenance and custody cases, evidence submitted by men is frequently overlooked, while a woman's statements are treated as unquestionable truth. In Family court every word of women is a Gospel Truth. Interim maintenance is granted swiftly, without trial or evidence, and courts rarely verify whether the woman is employed or if she left the marriage of her own accord. Maintenance is often awarded solely based on a domestic violence claim, without thorough scrutiny of the circumstances.

Women receive free legal aid, the law favours them, and they can file cases at no cost. Numerous legal provisions are designed to protect their interests, allowing them to misuse laws without facing any accountability for false cases. Even in extreme situations, such as when a woman kills her husband, she is still labelled the victim. Adultery laws do not apply to women, yet they can accuse their husbands of adultery without any proof-claims that courts often accept as valid grounds for awarding them maintenance and child custody. These are the stark realities of family courts.

Family courts consistently portray men as villains and criminals, with judges often mocking them. In a recent incident, someone recorded a judge's abusive remarks and shared them on social media, yet the person who exposed the misconduct was penalized-while the judge faced no consequences. Women receive free legal aid, whereas men must hire lawyers who drain them financially. It's not just the man who suffers; his entire family, including his mother and sisters, are treated as criminals the moment his wife files a case against him.

So, it is better to call Indian Family courts as "**slaughterhouses**" or "**Gestapos**".

Maintenance – A reverse dowry

Maintenance.

Other than India, all over the world, there is a criteria to check balanced Alimony/Maintenance.

Alimony (also called spousal support or maintenance) in Western countries is typically decided based on factors that vary by jurisdiction, but common considerations include:

1. Length of the Marriage

Longer marriages generally result in higher or longer-duration alimony.

Short-term marriages may not qualify for alimony unless there are exceptional circumstances.

2. Income and Financial Disparity

If one spouse earns significantly more than the other, the lower-earning spouse may receive support to maintain a reasonable standard of living.

3. Standard of Living During Marriage

Courts often aim to allow both spouses to maintain a lifestyle similar to what they had during the marriage.

4. Earning Capacity and Career Sacrifices

If one spouse sacrificed career opportunities (e.g., staying home to raise children), they may receive alimony to compensate for lost earning potential.

5. **Age and Health of Both Spouses**

Older or ill spouses who cannot work may receive more support.

Younger, healthier spouses may be expected to become self-sufficient sooner.

6. **Parental Responsibilities** (Child Custody)

The spouse with primary custody may receive additional support, especially if they cannot work full-time due to childcare responsibilities.

7. **Contributions to the Marriage**

Contributions can be financial or non-financial (e.g., homemaking, supporting the spouse's career).

8. **Pre-nuptial or Post-nuptial Agreements**

If there was a valid agreement outlining alimony terms, courts may enforce it unless it's deemed unfair.

9. **Fault-Based vs. No-Fault Divorce**

In some jurisdictions, if one spouse committed adultery or misconduct, it might affect alimony (though many Western countries follow a no-fault system where marital misconduct doesn't impact support).

10. **Ability to Pay**

The paying spouse must have sufficient income or assets to provide alimony without suffering undue financial hardship.

11. Duration of Alimony

Temporary: Until the recipient spouse can become self-sufficient.

Permanent: In cases of long marriages or when the recipient cannot work.

Lump Sum: A one-time payment instead of ongoing support.

Rehabilitative: Support for a fixed period to allow the recipient to gain employment skills or education.

12. Cohabitation or Remarriage of Recipient

If the recipient spouse moves in with a new partner or remarries, alimony may be reduced or terminated.

Alimony, Indian women birth-right

None of these factors are considered in India when maintenance is decided. The primary criterion often seems to be simply that the applicant is a woman.

In India, when a woman gets married, she is not expected to bring any financial contribution, as dowry is legally prohibited. According to traditional cultural norms, it is the man's responsibility to build and provide a home. If a couple has no roof over their heads, society and the law place the burden solely on the man.

Expecting a woman to contribute equally toward building a home is even considered cruelty under Indian law. A man cannot legally demand or expect such a contribution from his wife.

As of 2024, approximately 41.7% of Indian women aged 15 and above are part of the labor force, according to the Ministry of Labour and Employment. This marks a significant increase from 23.3% in 2017–18, indicating a notable rise in women's participation in economic activities across both rural and urban areas.

Out of the 41% of employed women in India, fewer than 2% are known to contribute equally toward building a home. Despite growing female workforce participation, financial responsibilities within marriages remain heavily skewed.

In most Indian households, men continue to bear the bulk of expenses—from buying or renting a house to paying monthly bills. There's an old Indian saying: "What's hers is hers, and what's his is also hers." This mindset still prevails.

Beyond financial upkeep, men are also expected to buy gold for their wives, fund family events, and provide material comforts. In return, societal expectations of women remain vague or minimal when it comes to financial contribution.

If a man suggests reversing roles—offering to handle cooking and household chores while the woman becomes the sole breadwinner and buys the house—he'd likely find very few women willing to accept that arrangement.

Traditionally, a bride's family would visit a potential groom's home to see if there is salt in the kitchen or livestock in the yard. Today, they assess the size of his house, whether he owns a car, and if domestic help is available.

In India, demanding dowry during marriage is illegal, but when a marriage ends through separation or divorce, a man is legally obligated to pay alimony or maintenance to his wife. While dowry is prohibited, this form of "reverse dowry" is considered a legal right for women. A man cannot refuse or object to paying maintenance, even if he finds his wife with another man or Lover, as the law enforces his duty to provide financial support.

Tools of Harassment

Harassment in marriage, whether by wives or husbands, often involves emotional, verbal, or psychological tactics that erode trust and well-being. The behaviors listed below — threats of suicide, insulting parents, withholding sex, flaunting affairs, or going out with lovers—can indeed constitute daily harassment when used to control or demean. Adding to this, verbal abuse, financial control, and public humiliation are common tactics that further strain relationships.

Emotional & Psychological Abuse

- Threatening Suicide to manipulate the husband emotionally or force compliance.
- Guilt-tripping or blackmailing over small issues, constantly making the husband feel at fault.
- Silent treatment, ignoring for days to assert control or punishment.
- Public humiliation, shaming the husband in front of family, children, or on social media.
- Using guilt, silent treatment, or mood swings to control the husband's behavior, e.g., ignoring him for days to "punish" minor disagreements.

Verbal & Mental Torture

- Consistent belittling, mocking, name-calling, or abusive language.
- Bringing up past mistakes repeatedly to lower self-esteem.
- Insulting husband's parents, mocking their status, or demanding they be kicked out or sent to old age homes.
- Regular insults, name-calling, or demeaning comments about the husband's appearance, job, or abilities (e.g., "You're useless, you can't even earn enough"). This chips away at self-worth.

Sexual Manipulation

- Withholding sex or affection as a punishment or control tactic. Husband is only to pay her bills, most Indian women treat husband as an ATM.
- Openly having an affair, talking to or meeting a lover in front of the husband.
- Going out with lovers without consent or consideration, sometimes even boasting about it.
- Lack of active participation or emotional connection during intimacy—such as lying motionless, showing indifference, or adopting a 'do it yourself' attitude—can deeply impact a man's emotional well-being. Additionally, making hurtful remarks about his body or performance, like criticizing size or labeling it

a 'quickie,' can damage his self-esteem and gradually erode his confidence and libido.

Controlling Behavior

- **Financial control**: demanding full salary, not allowing the husband to manage his own expenses. Stop husband from helping or giving money to his old aged Parents.
- Controlling interactions with friends, family, and even work colleagues.
- Using children to manipulate or threaten, e.g., threatening to take custody or turn them against the father.
- **Excessive Demands**: Setting unrealistic expectations, like demanding constant attention or perfection in household duties, and berating him for falling short.
- Criticizing or mocking the husband in front of friends, family, or on social media to shame him and assert dominance.
- **Gaslighting**: Denying or twisting events to make the husband doubt his reality, e.g., "I never said that, you're imagining things," to avoid accountability.

List of Behaviors and Their Impact:

Threat of Suicide:

Some spouses may threaten self-harm to manipulate or control their partner, creating fear and guilt. For example, saying, "If you don't do what I want, I'll kill myself," can place immense emotional pressure on the husband, forcing compliance to avoid perceived consequences.

Impact: This can lead to anxiety, emotional exhaustion, and a sense of being trapped, as the husband may feel responsible for their spouse's well-being.

Insulting Husband's Parents or Forcing Their Removal:

A spouse might belittle or mock their husband's parents, targeting their character, habits, or role in the family. For instance, making derogatory remarks like, "Your parents are a burden," or pressuring the husband to send them to an old-age home or cut contact.

In some cases, this can escalate to demands that the husband choose between the spouse and his parents, creating familial rifts.

Impact: This undermines the husband's familial bonds, causing guilt, stress, and conflict, especially in Indian households where joint families are common.

Withholding Sex:

Deliberately refusing intimacy as a form of punishment or control, such as saying, "You don't deserve me because you didn't do X," can be a way to manipulate or express resentment.

This differs from personal choice or mutual consent, as it's used to assert power rather than reflect genuine disinterest or comfort levels.

Impact: Can lead to feelings of rejection, inadequacy, or frustration, damaging emotional and physical intimacy in the marriage.

Openly Having an Affair and Talking to Lover in Front of Husband:

Engaging in extramarital relationships and flaunting them, such as taking calls with a lover or discussing the affair openly to taunt the husband, can be a form of emotional abuse. For example, saying, "He's better than you," to provoke or humiliate.

Impact: This erodes trust, self-esteem, and mutual respect, often leaving the husband feeling powerless or betrayed.

Going Out with Lovers Without Husband's Consent:

A spouse might leave the home to meet a romantic partner, disregarding the husband's feelings or the marital commitment, sometimes announcing it to challenge his authority, e.g., "I'm going out, and you can't stop me." As in India husband can't charge wife for Adultery.

Impact: This can cause public humiliation, emotional pain, and a sense of disrespect, particularly in cultures where marital fidelity is highly valued.

Important Notes:

These behaviours, are forms of abuse, and no one—man or woman—should have to live under that stress. If anyone find above said factors in your marriage then you are in Toxic relation.

Men often don't speak up due to social stigma or fear of not being believed. Women can be skilled at fabricating false narratives to elicit sympathy, even when their husband or partner is the actual victim of domestic abuse.

Contextual Notes:

Cultural Factors: In India, societal expectations around marriage, gender roles, and family dynamics can amplify the impact of these behaviours. For instance, insulting parents or pressuring their removal is particularly charged in joint-family setups. However, these issues aren't unique to Indian wives and can occur across cultures or genders.

Escalation to Legal Threats: Mentioned behaviours like threatening false 498A (dowry harassment), DV (domestic violence), or marital rape cases. Even without filing, threatening such actions can be a form of daily harassment, used to intimidate or coerce the husband into compliance due to the fear of legal or social consequences. Same threats sooner than later turn to be tools of Legal terrorism.

Misuse of Laws (Legal Harassment)

- **False cases of**:
- Section 498A IPC (Cruelty by husband or relatives)
- Domestic Violence Act (DV)
- Marital Rape (in states or cases where applicable)
- Threatening arrest, police complaints, or social ruin unless demands are met.
- Using the legal system as leverage in property disputes, divorce settlements, or child custody.

Understanding the Manipulation of Narrative in Abusive Relationships

The Concept: Fabricating a False Narrative

Most Women can be highly manipulative and capable of crafting false stories or exaggerated claims. When a woman does this in the context of a relationship where she is the abuser, the goal may be to:

- Elicit sympathy from friends, family, police, courts, or the public
- Discredit the husband or partner, painting him as violent, negligent, or emotionally abusive
- Preemptively control the narrative, especially in case of separation, divorce, or child custody disputes

How It Happens: Tactics Used

Emotional Storytelling:

- She might tell emotionally charged stories filled with half-truths, selective facts, or fabricated incidents.
- These stories often emphasize her pain, fear, or helplessness—even if she was the aggressor in the situation.

Playing the Victim in Public:

- Crying in front of relatives or friends to gain support.
- Posting emotional content on social media, hinting at being abused, abandoned, or mistreated.
- Portraying the husband as controlling or violent without any proof.

Pre-emptive Legal Strikes:

- Filing false domestic violence, dowry harassment (498A), or marital rape cases to strengthen her position in a separation or custody battle.
- Using these legal complaints to leverage financial settlements or alimony.

Manipulating Social Perception:

- Telling relatives, friends, neighbours or co-workers that she's in a bad marriage, ensuring if conflict arises later, people already side with her.

- Isolating the husband from his support system by accusing his family or friends of mistreating her.
- Telling her family, friends that her husband had an affair and he is neglecting her.

Gaslighting the Husband:

- Denying or minimizing her own abusive behavior.
- Twisting facts to make him question his memory or perception of reality.
- Making him feel guilty for things she initiated (e.g., provoking fights and then crying victim).

Why It's Effective:

- **Societal Bias**: Many people still find it hard to believe that a woman can be abusive or manipulative. Most think Women is victim always.
- **Legal System Limitations**: In India (and many countries), laws like Section 498A, DV Act, and maintenance laws are often heavily tilted in favor of women—and while meant to protect, they can be misused.
- **Emotional Impact**: People naturally want to protect someone who appears vulnerable or in distress.

Impact on the Actual Victim (the Husband)

- He may face character assassination, job loss, social isolation, or even jail time.
- He may become depressed, anxious, or suicidal due to the emotional and social toll.
- He may lose access to children, family, or even his own home.
- Often, his voice is ignored, and his attempts to defend himself are seen as aggression.

Important Clarification:

- Most women do this.
- Most women reporting abuse are not genuine victims.
- Mostly women misuse of protective laws and emotional manipulation in all cases.
- Men, too, deserve protection, fair hearing, and dignity.

Tools of Manipulation in Marital Disputes.

In recent years, there has been a growing discourse around the misuse of legal provisions by most women in the context of marital disputes. Manipulative false accusations being used as strategic tools to gain maintenance, child custody, or social advantage.

Alleging Extramarital Affairs Without Evidence

One of the most commonly reported false allegations is that the husband is involved in an extramarital affair. This accusation often serves multiple purposes:

- It discredits the husband's character in court and before family and society.
- It justifies the wife's decision to leave the matrimonial home without a valid reason.
- It paints her as a wronged woman, increasing her chances of receiving sympathy, interim maintenance, and custody of children.

Ironically, such accusations are sometimes made after the husband catches the wife in an inappropriate relationship—serving as a deflection strategy to avoid accountability and shift the focus of blame.

Accusing the Husband of Financial Neglect

Another tactic observed in many maintenance cases is the claim that the husband spends his earnings on his parents or siblings and neglects his wife and children. While in traditional Indian households, it is not uncommon for men to support their parents financially, this is often framed as "neglect" to project him as irresponsible.

This narrative ignores the fact that joint family responsibilities are culturally embedded in Indian society.

Courts often take such allegations at face value without asking for detailed financial records or proof of neglect.

The allegation becomes a convenient justification for seeking maintenance, even in cases where the wife may have deserted the husband or has her own income.

Claims of Domestic Violence and Substance Abuse

One of the most serious forms of false accusation is claiming that the husband comes home drunk and beats the wife and children, even when he is not a drinker at all.

Such accusations are hard to disprove, especially without eyewitnesses or medical records.

The mere filing of such complaints under Section 498A IPC or the Domestic Violence Act often leads to automatic legal consequences, including arrest or restraining orders.

Courts frequently grant interim relief based on these claims without demanding sufficient proof, further tilting the legal scale.

Alleging Incestuous Behaviour

Perhaps the most shocking and damaging false accusation reported in some rare but disturbing cases is the claim that a husband is involved in an incestuous relationship with his own mother or sister.

These baseless allegations aim to completely ruin the husband's credibility and character.

They often serve to justify the wife's desertion or her extramarital affair, portraying the husband as mentally or morally unfit.

In most of these cases, no proof is presented, yet the stigma sticks permanently.

Such accusations not only devastate the man emotionally but also damage the reputation and mental well-being of his entire family, often with no recourse or counter-justice.

Judicial Passivity and Presumption of Truth

A major concern in these cases is the lack of accountability or scrutiny from the judiciary. Indian courts often operate under the presumption that the woman is the victim, and her statements are treated as gospel truth—especially during interim hearings.

Rarely are women asked to prove their claims before being awarded maintenance or temporary child custody.

Men who raise doubts about these claims or submit evidence in their defense are often seen as aggressors or trying to "escape responsibility."

This one-sided assumption undermines justice and can encourage misuse of legal protections meant for genuine victims.

In India, the lack of checks and balances when it comes to verifying allegations made during matrimonial disputes has created a system that can be easily manipulated. Instead of requiring concrete evidence or conducting thorough investigations, family courts often act on the presumption that the woman is the victim—granting her interim maintenance, residence rights, or child custody without even questioning the authenticity of her claims. This approach not only undermines the principles of justice but incentivizes false accusations, turning them into powerful tools during separation or divorce proceedings.

What further fuels this issue is the standardized, almost mechanical approach taken by many legal practitioners. It is common practice for lawyers to maintain pre-drafted templates or "sample petitions"—filled with severe allegations such as domestic violence, dowry demands, emotional abuse, or neglect. These applications are often filed without customizing them to reflect the truth of a given situation, and are designed purely to maximize legal leverage for the woman. In contrast, husbands who are innocent or even victims themselves find it incredibly difficult to have their side of the story heard, especially in the early stages of litigation.

All these allegations made against the husband— ranging from infidelity to abuse and even incest—are often entirely false and baseless, yet the courts rarely challenge them. Despite the serious nature of such accusations, judges seldom initiate proceedings under Section 340 of the CrPC (which deals with perjury and false statements in judicial proceedings), nor do they hold the complainant accountable for proving her claims. This shifts the burden unfairly onto the man, forcing him to prove a negative—that he did not commit the acts he's accused of. In legal terms, this is not only unreasonable, it's almost impossible, because you cannot produce evidence of something that never happened. This reversal of the burden of proof violates the fundamental principles of justice and often leaves the innocent husband defenseless, stigmatized, and broken, both emotionally and socially.

False accusations not only destroy the life of the man but also erode the credibility of genuine victims, leading to mistrust in the system. A justice system that blindly believes one party without investigation is not a fair one.

As a result, the system that was originally built to protect vulnerable women is now being misused by some to gain undue advantage. This not only victimizes men unfairly but also dilutes the credibility of genuine cases, making it harder for real victims to get the justice they deserve.

MyNation Hope Foundation reviewed over 500 petitions and applications filed by the wives of its members, and found a disturbing pattern: in nearly every case, the wife had accused her husband of having an extramarital affair, engaging in sexual relations with his own mother or sister, and labelled him as an alcoholic and beating her, even he is not

drinking also, regardless of whether there was any
supporting evidence.

Crimes by Indian women

Crimes by Indian Women: A Silent Epidemic

Crime has no gender, yet the legal and societal narrative in India often portrays women solely as victims, ignoring their role as perpetrators. While crimes committed by men are widely discussed and condemned, offenses committed by women remain underreported, overlooked, or even justified under the guise of self-defence, emotional distress, or provocation. This imbalance has led to a dangerous misconception that women are incapable of committing serious crimes-an assumption that not only distorts justice but also allows many female offenders to escape accountability.

Women as Perpetrators of Crime

The belief that women are inherently non-violent is not only misleading but also factually incorrect. Numerous studies and crime records indicate that women are involved in various types of offenses, including homicide, domestic violence, child abuse, financial fraud, and false legal cases aimed at extortion or revenge.

1. **Murder and Domestic Homicide**

   - According to crime data, over 600 husbands are murdered by their wives every year in India. However, these cases seldom receive not the same public or legal scrutiny as crimes where men are the accused. All these murders and crimes list can be found on Twitter/X Platform with hash tag, **#CrimeByIndianWomen**

- Cases of contract killings orchestrated by wives to eliminate their husbands for financial gains, extra-marital affairs, or property disputes have been steadily rising.

2.   **False Allegations as a Legal Weapon**

- The misuse of laws like Section 498A (Dowry Law), the Domestic Violence Act, and Rape Laws has led to the wrongful incarceration of thousands of innocent men.
- Women have increasingly used false allegations as a means to blackmail, harass, or extort money from husbands and in-laws.
- A significant percentage of rape and POCSO cases filed are later found to be fabricated, yet the accusers face no legal repercussions.

3.   **Domestic Violence Against Men**

- Domestic abuse is often assumed to be a crime where men are the perpetrators, but studies suggest that men too suffer from physical, emotional, and financial abuse at the hands of their wives.
- Many men endure verbal humiliation, economic coercion, false threats of legal action, and even physical violence, yet there are no dedicated laws to protect them.

4.   **Child Abuse and Parental Alienation**

- Women are not only capable of committing child abuse but also play a significant role in parental alienation, where fathers are falsely accused and separated from their children.
- Many mothers misuse child custody laws, using children as leverage to harass their former spouses by filing False POCSO cases.

5. **Abetment to Suicide**

- Several cases have emerged where men, unable to bear the relentless legal harassment, societal stigma, and financial ruin, have taken their own lives.
- Suicide notes left behind by victims often mention the direct role of their wives, in-laws, and legal exploitation, yet the law rarely holds these women accountable.

Legal System's Bias and Injustice

Despite the increasing number of crimes committed by women, the Indian legal system continues to be heavily skewed in their favour:

- Women who commit the same crimes as men receive lighter punishments or are acquitted due to societal sympathy.
- Even when convicted, female criminals are often portrayed as victims of circumstances rather than as offenders.
- There is no legal framework to protect men from domestic violence, false cases, or financial

exploitation, leading to an alarming rise in male suicides.

The Struggles of Abused Male Victims

Men who face domestic violence or emotional abuse find it nearly impossible to escape their situations due to:

1.   **Lack of Support** - There are no helplines, shelters, or support groups for abused men.

2.   **Fear of Losing Their Children** - Men stay in abusive marriages because courts almost never grant them custody of their children.

3.   **Judicial Bias** - Even if men prove they are victims, the legal system sides with women in almost all cases.

Many men act as shields between their abusive wives and their children, taking the physical or emotional abuse themselves to protect their kids. Yet, if they seek legal protection, they are either mocked or ignored.

Preventing Crime by Addressing Men's Issues

Crime is influenced by multiple factors such as socio-economic struggles, societal pressures, and lack of support systems. While many laws focus on preventing crime by supporting women, there is no initiative to help struggling men, which can lead to:

- Mental health deterioration
- Unemployment-driven desperation
- Suicides due to false cases or financial ruin
- Providing basic support for men-such as legal safeguards, mental health counselling, and financial aid-can prevent many petty crimes and help men stay on the right path.

Unmasking a Fraud and Bias.

Money making Gender Politics

The claim that the Gender Budget allocation in the Union Budget 2025-26 has increased to 8.86% (Rs 4.49 lakh crore) from 6.8% (Rs 3.27 lakh crore) in FY 2024-25 is accurate, as confirmed by multiple sources, including the Ministry of Women and Child Development and media reports. This 37.25% increase reflects a record-high commitment to women and girls' welfare, with 49 Ministries/Departments and 5 Union Territories contributing, up from 38 Ministries/Departments in 2024-25.

The Gender Budget Statement (GBS) is divided into

- Part A (100% women-specific schemes, Rs 1,05,535.40 crore, 23.50%),
- Part B (30-99% for women, Rs 3,26,672 crore, 72.75%), and
- Part C (below 30%, Rs 16,821.28 crorc, 3.75%).

The WCD Ministry leads with 81.79% of its budget dedicated to women initiatives, followed by Rural Development (65.76%) and Food & Public Distribution (50.92%). Key schemes include Saksham Anganwadi, POSHAN 2.0, and Mission Shakti, focusing on nutrition, safety, and economic empowerment.

The Misallocation of WCD/NCW Grants

For the past three to four decades, the Ministry of Women and Child Development (WCD) and the National Commission for Women (NCW) have been pivotal institutions in India's quest to empower women. These bodies, tasked with formulating policies, implementing schemes, and advocating for women's rights, reportedly receive substantial annual grants—often cited in public discourse as amounting to Rs 100,000 crore. However, despite these colossal allocations, the empowerment of Indian women remains elusive for many. A significant portion of these funds is allegedly siphoned off by fraudulent non-governmental organizations (NGOs) and corrupt officials, leaving grassroots women—especially in rural and marginalized communities—largely unaffected by the intended benefits. This essay critically examines the claim that massive WCD/NCW grants have failed to empower Indian women, exploring the role of fraudulent NGOs, systemic corruption, and structural inefficiencies, while proposing solutions to ensure funds reach their intended beneficiaries.

The Scale of Funding and Its Intended Purpose

The WCD Ministry, established as a department in 1985 and upgraded to a ministry in 2006, is the nodal agency for women and child welfare in India. It oversees schemes like Mission Shakti, Beti Bachao Beti Padhao, and the Support to Training and Employment Programme (STEP), aimed at promoting women's safety, education, and economic independence. The NCW, a statutory body formed in

1992, advises the government on women-related policies and addresses grievances, focusing on issues like dowry, domestic violence, and workplace harassment. Together, these institutions are entrusted with transforming the socio-economic status of Indian women, particularly the 70% living in rural areas who face systemic barriers to empowerment.

The claim that WCD and NCW receive Rs 100,000 crore annually is a point of contention. Official budgets indicate that the WCD Ministry's allocation for 2023-24 was approximately Rs 25,172 crore, with schemes like Saksham Anganwadi and POSHAN 2.0 (81%) and Mission Shakti (12%) dominating the expenditure. NCW's budget, as an autonomous body, is significantly smaller, around Rs 258 crore alongside other bodies like the Central Adoption Agency. The figure of Rs 100,000's crore symbolic amount, but it reflects public perception of vast resources allocated to women's empowerment. Regardless of the exact amount, the critical issue is that these funds have not translated into proportional outcomes, raising questions about their utilization.

The Plague of Fraudulent NGOs

A significant barrier to effective fund utilization is the proliferation of fraudulent NGOs. In 2015, the media reported a shocking finding by the WCD Ministry: nearly 90% of 1,400 NGOs applying for grants under the STEP scheme, with a corpus of Rs 30 crore, were fake. These organizations submitted false names, fabricated details, or applied multiple times to siphon funds. This was not an isolated incident. A 2018 NCW report on Swadhar Greh, a scheme providing shelter homes for women, revealed that Rs 200 crore allocated to NGOs in states like Uttar Pradesh and Karnataka was misused. Shelters were found operating as hostels, charging fees to non-destitute women, or housing men on the same premises, posing safety risks.

According to senior WCD Ministry officials, of the 1,400 to 1,500 applications received, the vast majority were found to have submitted false names, fabricated details, or applied multiple times to siphon funds. This revelation underscored a critical failure in the vetting process and highlighted the audacity of fraudulent entities exploiting a system meant to serve the disadvantaged.

Causes of the Proliferation of Fake NGOs

Several factors contribute to the alarming prevalence of fake NGOs under schemes like STEP. First, the lack of stringent oversight and verification mechanisms allowed fraudulent organizations to infiltrate the system. The WCD Ministry's scrutiny process, while eventually effective in identifying fakes, was reactive rather than preventive, indicating a gap in initial application screening. Many NGOs provided misleading information, such as fictitious addresses or exaggerated claims of past work, which went undetected until a thorough investigation was conducted.

Second, the allure of government funding creates a fertile ground for opportunists. With a Rs 30 crore corpus, STEP represents a significant financial opportunity for unscrupulous entities. The absence of robust monitoring post-fund allocation further emboldened fake NGOs to exploit the system, knowing that their activities might not be closely scrutinized.

Third, the broader socio-economic context plays a role. India's vast and diverse NGO sector, with over 230,000 registered non-profits, operates in a landscape where poverty and inequality drive the need for social interventions. This demand creates a perception that NGOs are a quick route to funding, attracting fraudulent players who masquerade as legitimate organizations. As noted in a 2013 Delhi High Court observation, 99% of NGOs were deemed **"fraudulent"** or **"money-making devices,"** suggesting that the issue extends beyond the WCD scheme to the entire sector.

The ease with which fake NGOs infiltrate government schemes stems from weak vetting processes. Many NGOs exploit the demand for grassroots interventions by presenting falsified credentials, knowing that initial scrutiny is often superficial. The WCD Ministry's decision to publicly list fake NGOs was a reactive measure, but it highlighted a deeper issue: the lack of proactive, technology-driven verification systems. For instance, platforms like the Darpan Portal, meant to register NGOs, are underutilized for real-time cross-checking. This systemic loophole allows fraudulent entities to divert funds meant for skill training, shelter, or rehabilitation, leaving genuine NGOs and beneficiaries underserved.

Corruption and Political Misconduct

Corruption within the administrative and political machinery exacerbates the misallocation of funds. High-profile scandals involving cabinet ministers and chief ministers, such as the 2010 Commonwealth Games scam (Rs 70,000 crore) and the Coal Mining Scam (Rs 1.86 lakh crore), illustrate the pervasive nature of corruption in India. While these are not directly tied to WCD/NCW, they reflect a broader culture of impunity that permeates public fund management. A 2005 Transparency International study found that over 62% of Indians had paid bribes to public officials for services, indicating systemic corruption at all levels.

Within the WCD context, underutilization of funds is a recurring issue. A 2021 parliamentary panel report criticized the WCD Ministry for "gross underutilization" of funds under flagship schemes like Beti Bachao Beti Padhao, where only 25% of Rs 848 crore allocated from 2014-15 to 2019-20 was spent by states. Similarly, Mission Shakti saw a 36% gap between budgeted and actual expenditure in 2021-22. Such underutilization often masks diversion of funds or bureaucratic delays, with corrupt officials allegedly pocketing money through ghost beneficiaries or inflated project costs. The 2018 Swadhar Greh scandal, where NGOs manipulated women to stay in shelters for continued funding, suggests complicity by local officials who failed to monitor operations.

Political interference further complicates matters. The NCW has faced accusations of bias, notably in 2025 when the Trinamool Congress labelled it a "political wing of the BJP" during a visit to riot-affected Murshidabad. Such politicization undermines the NCW's credibility, diverting attention from its core mandate. Corrupt ministers or officials may prioritize loyal NGOs or regions, side-lining genuine organizations and perpetuating a cycle of inefficiency.

The Real Question: Gender Equality or Gender Bias?

The real issue isn't just about whether fraud or corruption exists—what's undeniable is that the Gender Budget allocation exclusively for women in the Union Budget 2025–26 stands at Rs.4.49 lakh crore. This is a fact that cannot be disputed.

But this raises some important questions:

- How much has been allocated exclusively for men?

- Are there any government schemes designed specifically for men?

- Despite substantial funding, numerous welfare schemes, freebies, and reservations—why is it that women are still said to be "not empowered"?

- Why do many women still beg for maintenance?

- And on the other hand, how are men expected to be "empowered" when there are no exclusive funds or targeted welfare schemes for them?

- Where all funding of women goes?

These questions deserve honest reflection if we are truly striving for equality, not selective empowerment.

India Vs. West

In Western countries, women's empowerment was achieved through education, equal treatment, and training, rather than relying on long-term funding, freebies, or reservation policies. Government funding was provided for a limited time, after which, the focus shifted to sustaining empowerment through equality.

In India, however, there's a continued emphasis on funding, reservations, and freebies, accompanied by blaming men, patriarchy and society, with funding amounts increasing annually. This raises questions about why women can't empower themselves without these measures, similar to how men do, Men are empowered without any funding's and reservations. The lack of scrutiny and continuous sanctioning of funds by the Indian government, along with the alleged exploitation of victimhood by women's organizations to secure funding, is concerning. The absence of thorough audits to ensure funds reach those in need also raises doubts.

Despite significant funding over the past half-century, issues persist, such as the presence of beggars in family courts and a lack of safe homes or shelters for women outside major cities. There are orphan children on the streets despite the funding. Instead of taking responsibility and empowering themselves through available opportunities, freebies and reservations, women continue to blame men and patriarchy for their problems.

Adding to this, the Women and Child Development (WCD) ministry and the National Commission for Women (NCW) portray women as victims, while women's organizations label them as destitute, and the legal system often brands them as helpless. This perpetuates a cycle that seems to perpetuate a flow of taxpayer money.

In summary, the approach to women's empowerment
in Western countries focused on education and
equality, while in India, there's a heavy reliance on
funding and reservations, which some argue may be
counterproductive. The continuous funding without
adequate scrutiny and the persistence of problems
faced by women raise concerns about the
effectiveness and potential misuse of resources.

The epidemic of male suicides

Determining the exact number of young Indian men who have committed suicide specifically due to harassment by their wives over the past five years is challenging due to limitations in available data. The National Crime Records Bureau (NCRB) reports categorize suicides under broad headings such as "family problems," "illness," and "marriage-related issues," without delving into specific causes like spousal harassment. Additionally, the term "family problems" encompasses a wide range of issues beyond marital conflicts.

Between 2015 and 2022, marriage-related issues accounted for 3.28% of male suicides. However, this category includes various sub-factors such as non-settlement of marriage, dowry disputes, extra-marital affairs, divorce, and others, making it difficult to isolate suicides directly resulting from harassment by wives.

Moreover, the NCRB's "Accidental Deaths and Suicides in India" report does not provide detailed breakdowns of suicide causes, further complicating efforts to pinpoint specific triggers like spousal harassment.

While there have been individual cases highlighting the issue, such as the suicide of a 40-year-old businessman in Delhi who reportedly faced harassment from his wife and in-laws, these instances are anecdotal and do not offer comprehensive statistical insights.

Suicide Statistics

In summary, the lack of granular data in official reports prevents a precise determination of how many young Indian men have taken their own lives specifically due to harassment by their wives in the last five years. The existing statistics on marriage-related suicides encompass a broad spectrum of causes, making it difficult to draw specific conclusions about the impact of spousal harassment alone.

Unfortunately, providing a precise, definitive number of young Indian men who committed suicide specifically due to harassment by their wives within the last 5 years is difficult. This is due to several factors:

Data Collection Complexity:

Suicide statistics are collected by the National Crime Records Bureau (NCRB) in India. While they provide data on suicides, assigning a single, exclusive cause like "harassment by wife" can be complex. Suicides often result from a combination of factors.

The NCRB provides data on "marriage related issues" as a cause of suicide, but this category encompasses various sub-factors, not solely harassment.

Social Stigma and Reporting:

- Social stigma surrounding male victims of domestic abuse can lead to underreporting.
- Legal complexities and societal biases can also affect how such cases are recorded.
- Defining "Harassment":
- "Harassment" can be subjective and difficult to quantify.

However, here are some key points from the search results that shed light on the issue:

Suicide Data (NCRB Data)

The NCRB data does provide information regarding suicides related to "marriage related issues". It is important to know that Marriage related issues is a category that includes many sub categories.

Reports indicate that while "family problems" are a major cause of suicides in India, "marriage-related issues" are also a significant factor.

It is also important to note that more men commit suicide in India than women.

Recent Cases and Concerns:

- Recent high-profile cases have brought attention to allegations of men being driven to suicide due to harassment by their wives and in-laws.

- These cases have also sparked discussions about the potential misuse of laws designed to protect women.
- Factors contributing to male suicides:
- It is stated that the main reason for male suicides is "family problems"
- Illness is the second largest cause.
- Marriage related issues is the third largest cause.

Suicide Issues

It's clear that harassment and marital issues are contributing factors to male suicides in India. The issue is complex and requires further attention.

There is no specific data available in the provided contexts that directly quantifies the number of young Indian men who committed suicide solely due to harassment by their wives over the last five years. However, broader context can be inferred:

- Marriage-related suicides accounted for 3.28% of male suicides between 2015 and 2022, with 26,588 men dying due to marriage-related issues, including harassment, extramarital affairs, and non-settlement of marriage.
- Divorce-related suicides (which could include harassment) were 287 men in 2020, slightly higher than the 264 women who died for the same reason.

- Extramarital affairs caused 724 male suicides in 2020, compared to 636 female suicides, though this does not specify if harassment was the direct cause.

While the exact number for harassment by wives is not specified, these figures provide context on the broader category of marriage-related suicides among men.

Women Vs. Men

Over the last decade, male suicide rates in India have consistently been higher than female suicide rates, with men accounting for a significantly larger proportion of suicide cases. Here's a detailed breakdown:

1. **Overall Suicide Rates**:

   - The suicide rate for men in India in 2019 was 14.10 per 100,000, while for women, it was 11.10 per 100,000.
   - This trend has been consistent, with men's suicide rates generally 25-30% higher than women's over the past decade.

2. **Number of Suicides**:

   - Between 2015 and 2022, an average of 1,01,188 men died by suicide annually, compared to 43,314 women.
   - In 2020, out of 153,052 suicides, 71,139 were women, and the majority were men.

3. **Age Group**:

- Young men (18-30 years) are particularly vulnerable, with social, financial, and family pressures being significant contributors.
- Women, while also affected, often face different societal pressures, including dowry-related harassment and marital discord, but these do not result in as high a suicide rate as men.

4. **Marriage-Related Suicides**:

- Marriage-related issues (e.g., harassment, extramarital affairs) accounted for 3.28% of male suicides between 2015 and 2022, with 26,588 men dying due to such reasons.
- In comparison, women suicides due to marriage-related issues were lower, though still significant.

Summary

Over the last 10 years, male suicides in India have consistently outnumbered female suicides, with men facing higher rates due to societal, financial, and family pressures. Women face different, yet significant, challenges, but their suicide rates remain lower compared to men.

Over the past decade, suicide rates in India have exhibited notable gender differences. According to a study published in The Lancet, the suicide death rate

(SDR) for males decreased from 20.9 per 100,000 population in 1990 to 15.7 per 100,000 in 2021. For females, the SDR declined from 16.8 per 100,000 in 1990 to 10.3 per 100,000 in 2021.

This trend indicates a more significant reduction in suicide rates among females compared to males over the past three decades. However, it's important to note that despite the decline, males continue to have a higher suicide rate than females in India.

Additionally, a study analysing data from 2014 to 2021 observed that the male-to-female ratio of suicides increased from 1.9 and 2.5 to 2.4 and 3.2, respectively. Family problems and health issues were identified as prominent reasons behind these suicides.

These statistics underscore the critical need for targeted mental health support and intervention strategies, particularly focusing on male populations and addressing family-related stressors.

NCRB statistics on male suicide

NCRB statistics of men's suicides compared to women's suicides between 2010 and 2022.

Gender-wise Suicide Statistics in India

(2010–2022)

Year	Total Suicides	Male Suicides	Female Suicides	Male Percent	Female Percent
2010	1,27,770	87,180	40,590	68.2%	31.8%
2011	1,35,585	91,528	44,057	67.5%	32.5%
2012	1,35,445	91,921	43,524	67.9%	32.1%
2013	1,34,799	91,528	43,271	67.9%	32.1%
2014	1,31,666	89,098	42,568	67.7%	32.3%
2015	1,33,623	88,135	42,340	66.0%	31.7%
2016	1,31,008	87,180	41,384	66.5%	32.4%
2017	1,29,887	88,997	41,997	68.5%	32.3%
2018	1,34,516	90,917	43,599	67.6%	32.4%
2019	1,39,123	97,613	41,510	70.2%	29.8%
2020	1,53,052	1,08,532	44,498	70.9%	29.1%
2021	1,64,033	1,18,979	45,026	72.5%	27.4%
2022	1,70,924	1,22,724	48,172	71.8%	28.2%

Key Insights from 2010 to 2022

Key Insights of 2010:

Men accounted for ~68.2% of total suicides, while women made up ~31.8%.

The male-to-female suicide ratio was approximately 2.15: 1, reflecting a significant gender disparity.

Family problems and illness were among the leading causes of suicides for both genders.

Key Insights of 2011:

Men accounted for ~67.5% of total suicides, while women made up ~32.5%.

The male-to-female suicide ratio was approximately 2.08: 1, continuing the trend of men being disproportionately affected.

Family problems and illness remained the leading causes of suicides for both genders.

Key Insights of 2012:

Men accounted for ~67.9% of total suicides, while women made up ~32.1%.

The male-to-female suicide ratio was approximately 2.11: 1, maintaining the trend of higher male suicides.

Family problems and illness continued to be the primary causes of suicides for both genders.

Key Insights of 2013:

Men accounted for ~67.9% of total suicides, while women made up ~32.1%.

The male-to-female suicide ratio was approximately 2.11: 1, continuing the trend of higher male suicides.

Family problems and illness remained the leading causes of suicides for both genders.

Key Insights of 2014:
Men accounted for ~67.7% of total suicides, while women made up ~32.3%.
The male-to-female suicide ratio was approximately 2.09: 1, reflecting the continued trend of higher male suicides.
Family problems and illness remained the leading causes of suicides for both genders.

Key Insights of 2015:
Men accounted for ~66.0% of total suicides, while women made up ~31.7%.
The male-to-female suicide ratio was approximately 2.08: 1, continuing the trend of higher male suicides.
Family problems and illness remained the primary causes of suicides for both genders.

Key Insights of 2016:
Men accounted for ~66.5% of total suicides, while women made up ~32.4%.
The male-to-female suicide ratio was approximately 2.06: 1, continuing the trend of higher male suicides.
Family problems, illness, and economic stress were among the leading causes of suicides for both genders.

Key Insights of 2017:
Men accounted for ~68.5% of total suicides, while women made up ~32.3%.

The male-to-female suicide ratio was approximately 2.12: 1, reflecting the continued trend of higher male suicides.
Family problems, illness, and economic stress were among the leading causes of suicides for both genders.

Key Insights of 2018:
Men accounted for ~67.6% of total suicides, while women made up ~32.4%.
The male-to-female suicide ratio was approximately 2.08: 1, continuing the trend of higher male suicides.
Family problems, illness, and economic stress were among the leading causes of suicides for both genders. This data highlights the ongoing gender disparity in suicide rates in India during 2018.

Key Insights of 2019:
Men accounted for ~70.2% of total suicides, while women made up ~29.8%.
The male-to-female suicide ratio was approximately 2.35: 1, reflecting a significant increase in the disparity compared to previous years.
Family problems, illness, and economic stress were the primary causes of suicides for both genders.

Key Insights of 2020:
Men accounted for ~71.2% of total suicides, while women made up ~28.8%.
The male-to-female suicide ratio was approximately 2.4: 1, showing a further increase in the disparity compared to previous years.
Family problems, economic stress, and illness were the primary causes of suicides for both genders.

Key Insights of 2021:
Men accounted for ~72% of total suicides, while women made up ~28%.
The male-to-female suicide ratio was approximately 2.52: 1, reflecting a continued increase in the gender disparity.
Family problems, illness, and economic stress were the primary causes of suicides for both genders.

Key Insights of 2022:
Men accounted for ~71.8% of total suicides, while women made up ~28.2%.
The male-to-female suicide ratio was approximately 2.55: 1, showing a continued gender disparity.
Family problems, illness, and economic stress were the primary causes of suicides for both genders.

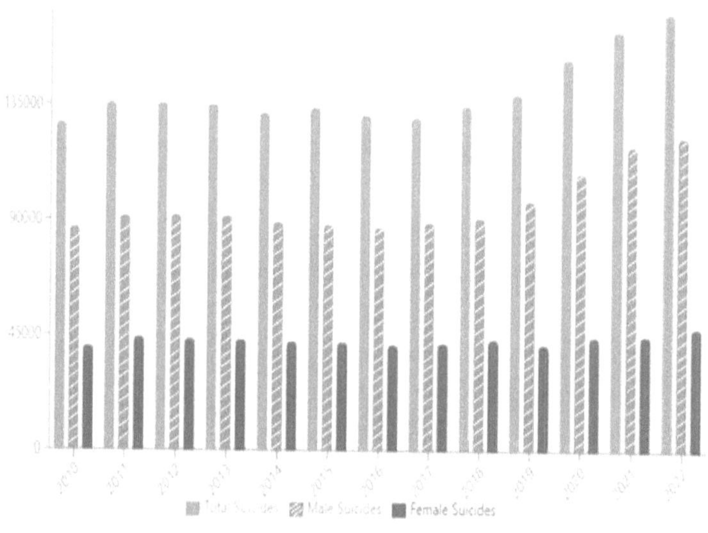

Fig:1- **Suicide statistics from 2010-2022**.

The statistics clearly indicate that men are dying by suicide at thrice the rate of women, yet government policies and legal protections remain disproportionately focused on women. Politicians, driven by vote-bank politics, continue to introduce laws and schemes favouring women while neglecting the struggles faced by men. This selective approach not only violates the equality clause of the Constitution of India but also reinforces a biased system that disregards the genuine needs of men this also promote Genocide of men. Instead of one-sided policies, there is an urgent need for a balanced and inclusive approach that recognizes and addresses the issues affecting men, ensuring true gender equality in both law and society.

Who needs Laws? Protection, Its MAN, not Women,
but only women has all the Laws and Protection,
Man has nothing.

The Legal Gap for Men

Indian law currently lacks adequate legal provisions to protect men from domestic violence. The Protection of Women from Domestic Violence Act (PWDVA) of 2005 was specifically enacted to safeguard women against various forms of domestic abuse, including physical, emotional, and economic violence. While this law was a significant step toward protecting women's rights, it does not account for situations where men may be victims of similar abuse. Unlike women, men do not have an equivalent legal framework that allows them to lodge complaints, seek protection orders, or claim relief under domestic violence laws.

The assertion that Indian men have no legal recourse against domestic violence, rape, or other forms of violence perpetrated by women, and that this lack of legal recognition results in the absence of relevant statistics from the National Crime Records Bureau (NCRB), presents a complex and sensitive issue. While the Indian legal framework has historically focused on protecting women from violence, the absence of gender-neutral laws in certain areas creates a disparity that warrants examination.

Rape and sexual assault laws in India also primarily focus on women as the victims, with the Indian Penal Code (IPC) Section 375 defining rape in terms of a man's non-consensual act towards a woman. The gendered language of the law restricts its application in cases where men might be victims of sexual violence, leaving such incidents outside the scope of formal legal recognition and response. Although there are some cases where men have been victims of rape or sexual assault, societal attitudes and the absence of gender-neutral laws make it difficult for them to report such crimes or to receive appropriate legal remedies.

It is true that specific sections of the Indian Penal Code (IPC), such as Section 498A (cruelty by husband or relatives), are primarily designed to protect women. This section, while intended to address the widespread issue of dowry harassment and domestic violence against women, does not offer reciprocal protection for men. This has led to concerns about its potential misuse and the lack of legal avenues for men who experience domestic abuse.

Similarly, the legal definition of rape under Section 375 of the IPC traditionally defines it as an act committed by a man against a woman. This definition has been challenged for its exclusion of male victims of sexual assault and female perpetrators. While recent legal interpretations and amendments have expanded the understanding of sexual violence, including recognition of male victims in certain contexts, the core definition remains gender-specific

Additionally, the concept of "cruelty" under IPC Section 498A, which addresses marital cruelty, is also gender-biased, with laws primarily designed to protect women from harassment by their husbands or in-laws. While men can theoretically be charged with cruelty under this provision, it is not commonly applied in practice. The assumption that men are perpetrators and women are victims limits the legal recourse for men facing cruelty, both physical and emotional, within marriage or intimate relationships.

However, it is inaccurate to say that men have *no* legal recourse. Men can file complaints under other sections of the IPC, such as those related to assault (Section 351), grievous hurt (Section 320), or criminal intimidation (Section 506), regardless of the perpetrator's gender. Moreover, other forms of violence, such as financial abuse or emotional manipulation, can be addressed through civil remedies.

The issue is not the complete absence of legal avenues, but rather the lack of specific, gender-neutral provisions that acknowledge and address the unique experiences of male victims of violence. This creates a significant gap in data collection and can lead to underreporting, as men may feel hesitant to report abuse if they believe their experiences are not legally recognized.

Several factors contribute to this situation, including societal norms and biases that often portray men as strong and invulnerable. These stereotypes can discourage men from seeking help and perpetuate the belief that they cannot be victims of abuse. Furthermore, the focus on protecting women from violence, while essential, has sometimes overshadowed the need to address violence against men.

The debate surrounding gender-neutral laws is complex and often contentious. Proponents argue that such laws are necessary to ensure equality and justice for all victims of violence, regardless of gender. They contend that the current legal framework perpetuates harmful stereotypes because feminist's propaganda, WCD, NCW influence on Politicians and others ignores the reality of male victimization.

The Social Stigma Surrounding Male Victims

One of the main reasons for the absence of legal provisions for male victims of domestic violence and other forms of abuse is the prevailing social stigma. There is a deep-rooted perception that men cannot be victims of domestic violence or sexual assault, as these issues are often framed within a traditional gendered lens. Cultural norms that associate masculinity with strength, control, and power create an environment where men may feel ashamed to report violence against them. Victims may fear ridicule, mockery, or disbelief from society and authorities, which prevents them from seeking help.

Moreover, the social expectation that men must always be the protectors and providers often lead to a sense of emasculation when they experience victimization. Such stigma discourages men from discussing their trauma or seeking the support they need. This silence, coupled with the absence of a supportive legal structure, further marginalizes the issue of male victimization.

The Impact of the Absence of Statistics

The absence of explicitly gender-neutral laws in these areas does contribute to the lack of comprehensive statistics on violence against men. The NCRB, which compiles crime statistics for India, primarily reports data based on existing legal definitions.

Therefore, if a crime is not formally recognized under a specific section of the IPC, its data collection becomes challenging

The lack of a legal framework for male victims of domestic violence, combined with the absence of accurate statistics, creates a vicious cycle of invisibility. Since the National Crime Records Bureau (NCRB) does not collect data on male victims of domestic violence, there is no official recognition of the problem. This makes it difficult to assess the magnitude of the issue, hindering policy changes and the creation of resources for male victims. The absence of this data also means that the government and civil society organizations cannot adequately respond to the needs of male survivors.

Furthermore, the unavailability of statistics prevents public awareness campaigns from addressing the issue of violence against men. While there are programs and NGOs focused on supporting female victims, there is a lack of similar infrastructure for men. The societal neglect of male victimhood contributes to their marginalization and deprives them of the resources they might need to heal.

The Need for Legal Reforms

To address the issue of male victimization in domestic violence and gender-based violence, there needs to be a comprehensive legal reform. First, laws should be amended to provide equal protection for both men and women. A gender-neutral approach to domestic violence, rape, and sexual assault would ensure that men who face violence in relationships have the same legal recourse as women. The Protection of Men from Domestic Violence Act could be considered, and modifications to existing laws would ensure that male victims are not left vulnerable.

Ultimately, addressing the issue of violence against men requires a multifaceted approach. This includes:

- **Legal reform:** Considering amendments to existing laws to ensure gender neutrality while maintaining protections for vulnerable groups.

- **Data collection:** Implementing mechanisms to collect accurate and comprehensive data on violence against men.

- **Public awareness:** Challenging societal stereotypes and promoting open dialogue about male victimization.

- **Support services:** Establishing support services specifically tailored to the needs of male victims of violence.

Additionally, the Indian Penal Code should be updated to reflect gender neutrality in its definition of rape, cruelty, and sexual assault. These changes would not only provide legal recourse for male victims but also help eliminate the stigma surrounding male victimhood. The NCRB should also begin collecting data on crimes committed against men, particularly in the context of domestic violence and sexual assault. Accurate statistics will allow for a more effective response and targeted interventions for male victims.

While the NCRB data may not fully capture the extent of violence against men due to existing legal frameworks, it is important to acknowledge that legal recourse exists for men, and the need for more comprehensive, gender neutral laws continues to be a topic of debate.

The lack of legal protections for men facing domestic violence, rape, and cruelty in India represents a significant gap in the country's legal and social systems. This absence of legal recourse, compounded by social stigma and the failure to collect relevant statistics, has marginalized male victims and left them without the support they need. To address this issue, there must be a shift toward gender-neutral laws that protect all victims of violence, regardless of their gender. Only then can India take a holistic approach to combating domestic violence and ensure justice for all, regardless of their gender.

The lack of accountability within the police and judiciary often forces men into prolonged struggles for justice, particularly in cases of legal terrorism initiated by their spouses. Police officers and judges frequently exercise discretionary powers that can be misused, leading to harassment and exploitation for financial gain. While there are mechanisms to address grievances, they are often ineffective when complaints originate from men. Police tend to prioritize cases filed by women due to directives from higher authorities, influenced by organizations like the WCD/NCW through government channels. Similarly, family court judges routinely deliver verdicts favouring women, often disregarding apex court guidelines. This systemic bias contributes to the alarming rate of male suicides, many of which are abetted by the actions of these judges. Yet, there is no accountability or functional mechanism to address judicial misconduct. A nexus between women's lawyers and judges further exacerbates the issue, with exaggerated maintenance claims frequently going unchallenged. When men attempt to file perjury applications (Sec.340 CrPC), judges dismiss them, claiming it would open a floodgate of litigation. The financial burden on men is immense, as they are forced to incur exorbitant legal fees, while women can file unlimited complaints free of cost, often with the sole intent of harassment. The apex court rarely scrutinizes these ground realities, occasionally issuing token guidelines that, more often than not, further disadvantage men. This systemic imbalance perpetuates a cycle of injustice, leaving men financially and emotionally devastated.

Indian society's bias against men is a multifaceted issue, rooted in outdated legal frameworks, cultural stereotypes, and institutional neglect. While women's empowerment is crucial, it must not come at the cost of men's exploitation. A balanced approach, recognizing and addressing the struggles of both genders, is essential for achieving true gender equality.

Indian society has long ignored these biases, assuming that men do not need protection or support. However, if true gender equality is to be achieved, it is essential to recognize and address the struggles faced by men.

The Urgent Need for Judicial Reform

The unchecked misuse of these laws has turned the Indian legal system into an institutionalized extortion racket, where men are often presumed guilty without evidence. The lack of legal safeguards against false accusations and the biased implementation of these laws have caused irreparable damage to thousands of innocent men and their families.

India's legal system must evolve to provide equal protection to both genders. The unchecked misuse of gender-biased laws has led to:

- Massive legal harassment of innocent men
- Destruction of families and careers due to false accusations
- Psychological trauma and suicides among falsely accused men

Conclusion

In India, domestic violence is often perceived as an issue affecting primarily women, with the legal framework geared towards their protection. The Domestic Violence Act (2005) and various sections of the Indian Penal Code (IPC) offer provisions for women who experience domestic abuse, rape, and cruelty. However, men who face similar forms of violence, including domestic abuse and rape, often find themselves without any legal recourse or support. This lack of a specific law for men has led to the absence of concrete statistics on the issue, even as men may also suffer from various forms of violence at the hands of women. Consequently, the National Crime Records Bureau (NCRB) does not collect statistics on **"cruelty against men,"** leaving this dimension of domestic violence largely unaddressed.

Tools of Legal Terrorism

How Dowry Law, Domestic Violence Law, Child Custody, Marital Rape / Rape, POCSO, and Maintenance Laws Have Become Tools of Legal Terrorism in India

Laws are meant to protect the vulnerable and ensure justice, but when misused, they can turn into weapons of extortion, harassment, and destruction. In India, several legal provisions designed to safeguard women have been systematically exploited, leading to devastating consequences for men and their families. These laws, instead of serving justice, have become tools of legal terrorism, enabling false accusations, financial exploitation, and the destruction of lives.

1. Dowry Law (Section 498A of IPC)

- Originally intended to protect women from dowry-related harassment, Section 498A of the Indian Penal Code has become one of the most abused laws in India.
- This law allows a woman to file a complaint of cruelty or dowry harassment, leading to the immediate arrest of the husband and his family members-even without any preliminary investigation.
- It is a non-bailable and non-compoundable offense, meaning once a case is filed, the accused must go through the lengthy legal process, regardless of the complaint's merit.

- Many women have misused this provision to settle personal scores, blackmail husbands, or force financial settlements.
- The Supreme Court of India itself has labelled the misuse of this law as legal terrorism, acknowledging the damage it has caused.

Dowry Law (Section 498A of IPC) - A Weapon of Legal Extortion

The Dowry Prohibition Act and Section 498A of the IPC were enacted to protect women from dowry harassment. However, these laws have been heavily misused due to their one-sided nature.

Case Study: An Innocent Family Destroyed

In 2000, Rudolph Dsouza (Author of this book), an IT Professional from Karkala Udupi, was falsely accused under Section 498A by his wife. He was arrested without investigation and Charge sheet was filed on the same day. Even after 25 years his Dowry case (Section 498A IPC) still running, quash of the case filed in 2013 at Bombay High Court, but his career was ruined, and his father passed away due to the stress of the case.

In 2017, Avnish B, a software engineer from Bangalore, was falsely accused under Section 498A by his wife. His entire family-including his 70-year-old mother and 75-year-old father-was arrested without investigation. After fighting a legal battle for three years, he was acquitted, but his career was ruined, and his father passed away due to the stress of the case.

Statistics on False Dowry Cases

- In 2022, the National Crime Records Bureau (NCRB) reported over 30% of 498A cases resulted in acquittals, proving they were false or unsubstantiated.
- In 2014, the Supreme Court of India stated that misuse of 498A was rampant, leading to unnecessary arrests and harassment.

2. Domestic Violence Law (DV Act, 2005)

- This law was meant to protect women from domestic abuse but is one-sided, offering no protection to men who face abuse from their wives.
- It allows women to claim residence rights and monetary compensation without requiring any proof of violence.
- Husbands are often forcibly evicted from their own homes based solely on accusations.
- The law is used as a tool for harassment, especially in divorce cases, where women file false complaints to gain leverage in legal proceedings.

Domestic Violence Law (DV Act, 2005) - Biased and Exploitative

This law provides only women with legal remedies, completely ignoring male victims of domestic violence.

Case Study: Suicide Due to False Domestic Violence Case

In 2019, Gaurav W, a 32-year-old banker from Mumbai, committed suicide after being falsely accused of domestic violence by his wife. In his suicide note, he wrote about the harassment he faced from his wife, her family, and corrupt police officers who demanded bribes to "settle" the case.

Statistics on Male Victims of Domestic Violence

- A 2018 survey by MyNation Hope Foundation found that over 52% of Indian men reported experiencing domestic violence but had no legal protection.
- NCRB data shows that over 1.7 lakh men commit suicide every year, with most linked to marital disputes.

3. Child Custody Laws (Guardian and Wards Act, 1890 & Hindu Minority and Guardianship Act, 1956)

- Courts overwhelmingly award child custody to mothers, assuming that they are the natural caregivers, even when fathers are equally capable of providing for and nurturing the child.
- Fathers are often reduced to mere visitors, with limited or no access to their own children.
- Many women use child custody as a bargaining chip in divorce settlements, demanding huge sums of money in exchange for visitation rights.
- This bias ignores the emotional and psychological trauma inflicted on both fathers and children who are deprived of a meaningful relationship.

Child Custody Laws - Fathers Reduced to Mere Visitors

Even when fathers are financially stable and emotionally involved, courts overwhelmingly grant child custody to mothers.

Case Study: A Father's 13-Year Battle for Custody, Paid 10 Lakhs for a Child Visit.

In 2013, Rudolph Dsouza (Author of this book), An IT professional from Karkala, Udupi, endured a gruelling 13-year legal battle to secure visitation rights for his son after his wife falsely accused him under the dowry law. Despite his relentless pursuit of justice, the Karnataka High Court granted him only limited visitation rights, and only after ordering him to deposit a staggering Rs.10 lakhs as a precondition for a single visit. This case starkly highlights the systemic bias and the immense financial and emotional toll faced by men entangled in false allegations.

Case Study: A Father's 10-Year Battle for Custody

In 2021, Rahul T, an IT professional from Pune, fought for 10 years to gain custody of his son after his wife falsely accused him of domestic abuse. Despite proving her extramarital affair, the court denied him custody, allowing only limited visitation rights.

Statistics on Child Custody Cases

- Over 90% of custody cases in India are awarded to mothers, ignoring the father's role in parenting.
- A 2020 Delhi High Court study found that shared parenting was ignored in 80% of cases, despite evidence showing its benefits for children.

4. False Rape and Marital Rape Allegations (Section 376 IPC)

- The rape laws in India have been framed with a "guilty until proven innocent" approach, where a mere accusation is enough to arrest a man, destroy his reputation, and ruin his career.
- False rape allegations are often used for personal vendetta, revenge, or financial

extortion, with little to no consequences for the woman if the claims are proven false.

- Women can file False rape case on any Man, even she has not seen or met. There was a case reported that a Women filed Rape case on a Man, as she complained that he raped her in her dream.

- There is a growing demand to criminalize marital rape, which, if implemented without safeguards, will give wives unrestricted power to file false cases against their husbands with no burden of proof required.

- If marital rape is criminalized without proper safeguards, every disagreement or dispute in a marriage can turn into a criminal case, leaving husbands defenceless.

False Rape and Marital Rape Allegations - Ruining Lives Without Evidence

Laws related to rape (Section 376 IPC) and sexual harassment are heavily biased against men, assuming guilt rather than innocence.

Case Study: False Rape Allegation Leads to Suicide

In 2018, Rohtak-based law student Anuj K was falsely accused of rape by his girlfriend after he refused to marry her. The case dragged on for two years, during which he lost his job and social reputation. Later, she admitted the case was false, but by then, Anuj had already committed suicide due to mental trauma.

Statistics on False Rape Cases

- A 2021 study by the Delhi Commission for Women found that 53% of rape cases in Delhi were false, filed due to personal vendetta or financial extortion.
- NCRB data shows that one in three rape cases filed in India results in acquittal due to false allegations.

5. **POCSO Act (Protection of Children from Sexual Offences Act, 2012)**

- While designed to protect minors from sexual abuse, this law is frequently misused in child custody battles, family disputes, and revenge cases.
- A single accusation under POCSO can destroy a man's life permanently, leading to arrests, job loss, and social stigma-even before the trial begins.
- In some cases, fathers have been falsely accused by estranged wives to ensure complete custody of the children.

POCSO Act (Protection of Children from Sexual Offences Act, 2012) - Used in Custody Disputes

The POCSO Act, meant to protect minors from sexual abuse, has been misused in child custody battles and revenge cases.

Case Study: A Father Wrongfully Accused of Molesting His Own Child

In 2020, software engineer Ramesh P from Hyderabad was accused of molesting his own daughter under POCSO by his estranged wife during a custody battle. After 2 years of legal trauma, he was acquitted, but his reputation was destroyed, and he lost access to his child permanently.

Statistics on False POCSO Cases

- A 2019 report by the Delhi High Court found that over 20% of POCSO cases were filed due to custody disputes or personal revenge.
- Many fathers never regain their reputation even after being acquitted.

6. Maintenance and Alimony Laws (Section 125 CrPC, HMA 24, 25)

- Men are forced to pay maintenance to their wives, even if the woman is well-educated, earning a salary, or capable of supporting herself.
- These laws do not take into account the financial burden on men, leading to economic ruin in many cases.
- Many women file for maintenance despite being in adulterous relationships or even after remarrying, exploiting legal loopholes to

continue receiving money from their ex-husbands.

- Maintenance laws are often weaponized as a financial extortion tool, making divorce an expensive and unfair process for men.

Maintenance and Alimony Laws - A System of Financial Extortion

Men are forced to pay maintenance to their wives, even if they are educated, capable of working, or at fault for the divorce.

Case Study: Man Ordered to Pay Maintenance Despite Wife's Affair

In 2017, Amit J, an entrepreneur from Bangalore, was forced to pay Rs.50,000 per month in maintenance, despite proving that his wife had an extramarital affair. The court ignored her adultery, ruling that she had a right to financial support.

Pradeep Singh Kanpur UP found himself entangled in a prolonged legal battle after discovering his wife's adultery just 43 days into their marriage. In response, she filed multiple police complaints across 11 stations in three states, accusing his family of dowry demands and domestic violence. Despite providing documented evidence, including marriage expense bills, he faced pressure from Gwalior Women's Cell to settle through compromise, followed by additional cases filed in Uttar Pradesh and a private complaint. The Allahabad High

Court stayed the proceedings, ordering mediation and Rs.15,000 deposit, which his wife accepted but then withdrew from mediation. She subsequently filed another complaint, leading to judicial custody and failed mediation sessions, during which her father reportedly threatened his life. Despite presenting evidence of her employment and adulterous behaviour, including a WhatsApp photograph with a 65B certificate, the judge ruled in her favour, citing mental cruelty and ordering maintenance based on the Supreme Court's judgment. Pradeep has endured six years of incessant travel 1800KM for every date and legal battles with minimal resolution.

Statistics on Maintenance Laws

- A 2019 study found that 70% of maintenance orders favoured women without verifying their financial independence.
- Courts rarely hold false complainants accountable, leading to rampant misuse of these provisions.

If Women Accuse man with Adultery without any evidence, that's valid in the eyes of Law, if Man produce evidence of his wife's Adultery that's counted as character assassination, out raging her modesty or Damage to her reputation.

PS: All above Laws specially designed for Women, only against Men.

What needs to Change?

Reforms

- **Gender-Neutral Laws** - Both men and women should be protected under domestic violence and sexual harassment laws. Laws on domestic violence, sexual assault, and harassment must apply to both men and women.
- **Strict Punishment for False Cases** - Filing false accusations should lead to severe legal penalties. Strict action should be taken against those who file false accusations.
- **Equal Child Custody Rights** - Courts must promote shared parenting rather than favouring one parent. Courts must ensure that fathers have equal parenting rights after separation.
- **Reform of Maintenance Laws** - Alimony should be based on need, not gender.
- **Presumption of Innocence** - No arrest should be made without a proper investigation in cases like 498A, rape, and POCSO.
- **Support Systems for Men** - Government and NGOs must establish helplines, counselling, and legal aid for men in distress.

Justice should be fair and unbiased, not a weapon of oppression. The fight for equal rights is not just a battle for men-it is a movement toward a just and balanced society.

Judicial & Law Enforcement Reforms

Strict Guidelines for Police & Judiciary

- Courts and police should scrutinize evidence before registering FIRs in sensitive cases.
- Arrests in matrimonial cases should only happen after proper verification.

Fast-Track Courts for Family & Marital Disputes

- Delay in cases allows misuse of the legal system as a weapon for harassment.
- Family courts should have strict timelines for resolving maintenance, divorce, and domestic violence cases.

Mediation & Counselling Before Legal Action

- Mandatory pre-litigation counselling should be enforced before allowing any criminal case under marriage laws.
- Mediation centres must be established to prevent unnecessary legal battles.

Social & Educational Reforms

Awareness About Legal Rights for Both Genders

- Legal literacy programs should educate both men and women about rights and responsibilities.

- Pre-marital legal counselling should be introduced to ensure awareness of marriage laws.

Promotion of Financial Independence for Women

- Encouraging women to be financially self-sufficient can reduce dependency and misuse of maintenance laws. Unless one sided alimony / Maintenance stopped no women is empowered.

Stigma Reduction for Victims of False Cases

- Society must stop blindly believing accusations and recognize the reality of false cases.
- Campaigns should highlight both genuine victims and victims of misuse.

Political & Policy Reforms

Formation of Ministry for Men

- A dedicated Ministry for Men's / Commission (similar to NCW) to address the legal and social issues faced by men.

Abolishing Lifetime Maintenance Without Justification

- Maintenance laws should not reward unemployment for an able-bodied spouse.
- Maintenance should be time-limited unless the spouse is genuinely incapable of earning.

- **Duration of Marriage as a Factor**: The length of marriage should be a critical consideration in determining maintenance. Short-lived marriages should not entitle a spouse to lifelong maintenance, as such arrangements often lead to exploitation rather than fairness..
- **Shared Parenting as a Standard**: To minimize litigation, shared parenting should be the default arrangement. Both parents should bear equal responsibility for raising their children, reducing the burden on one party and fostering a cooperative approach to child-rearing.
- **Time-bound Maintenance**: Maintenance should be restricted to a 6-month period, providing a reasonable window for the recipient spouse to secure employment or seek alternative means of support. Organizations like the WCD/NCW, which receive substantial annual funding (Rs.100,000 crore yearly), should step in to assist during this transitional phase, ensuring that the financial burden does not disproportionately fall on one individual.

Stricter Rules for Alimony Claims

- Courts should consider the woman's financial status before granting maintenance.
- Pre-marital and post-divorce assets of the husband should not be included in alimony calculations.

Conclusion

While laws to protect women are necessary, their misuse has created a system of legal terrorism that unfairly targets men and their families. A balanced approach with gender-neutral laws, stricter penalties for false cases, judicial reforms, and public awareness can help create a fair and just legal system in India.

Justice must be fair and unbiased, not a tool of harassment. Legal terrorism is a reality that needs urgent attention, and only through judicial reforms can true justice be achieved.

The misuse of these laws has created a legal system that disproportionately favours women, leaving men vulnerable to false accusations, financial exploitation, and social destruction. The absence of penalties for false cases and the presumption of guilt rather than innocence have turned these laws into tools of legal terrorism, destroying countless lives.

It is time for judicial reforms, gender-neutral laws, and stricter punishments for false allegations to ensure that justice is served fairly, rather than being used as a weapon for personal gain.

How Law protect Law misusers.

The Constitution of India guarantees equality and non-discrimination on the basis of gender through various provisions. The key provisions related to gender equality are:

Article 14 - Equality before the law:

- This article ensures that "the State shall not deny to any person equality before the law or the equal protection of the laws within the territory of India." It mandates that every individual, regardless of their gender, should be treated equally before the law.

Article 15 - Prohibition of discrimination on grounds of religion, race, caste, sex, or place of birth:

- This article prohibits discrimination on the basis of sex, among other factors. It means that the State cannot discriminate against individuals on the basis of gender in matters of public employment, education, or access to services.
- However, the article also allows for affirmative action or special provisions for women and children, which is intended to promote gender equality and provide for their welfare.

These constitutional provisions serve as the foundation for gender equality in India. The judiciary has also played a crucial role in interpreting as per Judges own beliefs and Interest, these provisions and expanding the scope of gender equality, often striking down discriminatory practices and laws as per constitution and imposed feminist's ideologies.

Adultery

- In India, adultery was historically considered a criminal offense under Section 497 of the Indian Penal Code (IPC). However, in a landmark judgment in 2018, the Supreme Court of India decriminalized adultery for both men and women. The court ruled that Section 497 was unconstitutional as it violated the right to equality and was discriminatory towards women.

- Prior to this ruling, Section 497 made adultery a punishable offense for men, but women were not directly punished under this law. Instead, the law focused on prosecuting the man involved in the adulterous act. The Supreme Court, in its decision, emphasized that the law was patriarchal and treated women as property, which was unjust and unfair.

- As a result of the 2018 ruling, adultery is no longer a criminal offense in India for either men or women, though it may still be grounds for civil actions such as divorce in family law matters.

- To summarize, adultery is not a punishable offense for women in India following the 2018 Supreme Court decision. So Court and Judges can make their Judgments violating Constitution, favouring Women.

- In another case, The Supreme Court of India, while hearing a divorce plea, came down heavily on a man for recording private conversations with his wife for years and using them as evidence in court. Evidence is Evidence, no matter how old and how it acquired, but when Man try to prove himself Innocent with evidence of Wife/Woman's extra marital Affairs, Wrong doings, As per Indian Feminists courts and Kangaroo courts that's not valid.

Key points of Section 122:

- The court will examine the applicability of Section 122 of the Indian Evidence Act, which protects communications between married couples. Under this section, a spouse is generally barred from revealing such conversations unless the evidence is submitted in a legal dispute between the spouses.

- Confidential Communication: It protects confidential communications made during the course of the marriage, ensuring that neither spouse can be compelled to reveal such private information in court.

- Spousal Privilege: The communication between a married couple is considered privileged, meaning the law recognizes the importance of preserving marital privacy and does not force a spouse to disclose sensitive or confidential discussions.

- Consent Required for Disclosure: The section allows for such communication to be disclosed in court only if the other spouse gives consent. Without the consent of the spouse who made the communication, it cannot be presented as evidence in court.

Limitations and Clarifications:

- The provision does not cover every type of communication within the marriage. It is specific to communications made during the course of the marriage that are considered confidential.
- The law aims to preserve the privacy and trust in a marital relationship by ensuring that sensitive communications are not exposed without consent.
- This provision, while not directly addressing privacy in a broad sense, protects marital confidentiality and ensures that spouses' communications remain private within the legal framework of the Indian Evidence Act.
- If Women submit the same that's Valid, but Man should not produce anything which make Women guilty. That's how Indian Courts, Protecting Adulators Women, Promoting extra marital Affairs in Marriage in Violation of Constitution of India.
- This is just an Example how Laws protect Women and her Interest, Indian Laws served in the best Interest of Women, not as per constitution or equality.
- In India, women can file multiple false cases against men without substantial proof, and their statements are often taken at face value in courts, her every word is Gospel truth for Indian Law, and Judges. The burden of proof falls entirely on the man, who has to spend lakhs of rupees gathering evidence and paying

legal fees. Lawyers often take advantage of this, demanding hefty payments but failing to represent their clients properly. In many cases, once a lawyer is fully paid, they may neglect the case, leaving the accused to struggle not only against the false allegations but also against his own legal counsel.

- Even after years of legal battles, if the man is acquitted, there is little to no punishment for the woman who filed the false case. Even when courts recognize that a case was filed with malicious intent, the penalty is often as low as Rs.200-Rs.500, while the accused may have spent Rs.2-Rs.3 lakhs or more in legal expenses. There are almost no legal options for a man to take an action against a negligent lawyer, as most lawyers refuse to file cases against their peers.
- This is the harsh reality of the Indian legal system-where false cases can ruin a man's life, drain his resources, and leave him with no real justice even after proving his innocence.

This is harsh reality of Indian Men, it's not only **LEGAL TERRORISM**, but its **STATE SPONSORED GENOCIDE**.

Case Studies

The Martyrs of legal terrorism

There have been several cases in India where men have taken their own lives due to alleged harassment through legal misuse, particularly under Section 498A IPC (dowry harassment cases), domestic violence laws, and maintenance/alimony disputes. Many have left behind suicide notes or videos explaining their distress.

Notable Cases of Men Who Died by Suicide Due to Legal Terrorism.

1. **Mohit Tyagi**:

   - A 34-year-old man from Ghaziabad, Uttar Pradesh who died by suicide on 17th April 2025. In his letter a suicide note accused his wife and her Brother and other family for harassment, continues torture and mental torture.

2. **Nishant Tripathi**:

   - A 41-year-old man from Mumbai who died by suicide in March 2025. He uploaded a suicide note to his company's website, blaming his wife and her aunt for harassment, before hanging himself in a hotel room.

3.   **Manav Sharma**:

- A techie from Agra who died by suicide in February 2025. He recorded a seven-minute video with a noose around his neck, highlighting his struggles and calling for laws to protect men, blaming his wife for harassment.

4.   **Atul Subhash**:

- A 34-year-old software engineer from Bengaluru who died by suicide in December 2024. He left a 24-page suicide note and an 81-minute video alleging harassment by his estranged wife, her family, and judicial misconduct during divorce and custody disputes.

5.   **Sandeep Paswan**:

- A young man who died by suicide in December 2024. He reportedly left a video or note expressing his distress, though specific details about his case are less documented in the provided references.

6.   **Harish** (Sub Inspector):

- A sub-inspector who took his life in December 2024, mentioned in X posts. He left behind a note or video crying out for justice, though detailed circumstances are not widely reported in the sources.

7.   **Deepanshu** (Professor):

- A professor who committed suicide in December 2024. He left a note or video expressing his grievances, but specific details remain limited in the available data.

8.   **Akshay Waghmare** (Pune, 2023)

- A 35-year-old man recorded a video before ending his life, blaming false dowry and domestic violence cases filed by his wife.

9.   **Manish Gupta** (Uttar Pradesh, 2022)

- A businessman left a suicide note citing harassment from his wife and in-laws due to a false dowry case.

10.   **Amit Kumar**:

- An IT worker who died by suicide in 2022 (exact date unclear from sources). He left a four-page note claiming his character was tarnished by workplace allegations, leading to charges against colleagues for abetment.

11.   **Dr. Archit Bhatt** (Gujarat, 2021)

- A doctor left a note before suicide, accusing his wife of continuous mental harassment through false legal complaints.

12.   **Jasmeet Singh** (Delhi, 2020)

- A software engineer recorded a video message before taking his life, blaming the misuse of domestic violence laws by his wife.

13.   **Gaurav Chandel** (Noida, 2019)

- An entrepreneur wrote a detailed letter about being falsely accused in multiple maintenance and domestic abuse cases, leading to financial ruin.

14.   **Shailesh Rajput** (Madhya Pradesh, 2018)

- A young man left a note stating he could not fight a false dowry case and was facing extreme stress.

15.   **Amit Bansal** (Punjab, 2017)

- A teacher took his life, leaving behind a letter mentioning false accusations and extortion through legal cases.

16.   **Mukesh Pandey**(Delhi, 2017):

- The Buxar district magistrate who died by suicide in August 2017 in Delhi NCR. He left a five-minute video discussing the futility of life and mentioning frequent quarrels with his wife, though he stated no one should be held legally responsible.

17.   **Sandeep Gupta** (Mumbai, 2016)

- A banker ended his life, citing his wife's legal threats and blackmail through misuse of women-centric laws.

18.   **Vikas Sharma** (Jaipur, 2014)

- A businessman left behind a video explaining how he was falsely implicated in a domestic violence case, leading to his suicide.

Common reasons in These Cases

- False dowry & domestic violence allegations leading to arrests without investigation.
- Financial ruin due to maintenance/alimony laws.

- Social stigma & loss of reputation.
- Custody battles where fathers were denied access to their children.

These incidents highlight the urgent need for legal reforms to prevent misuse of gender-biased laws and ensure justice for all.

In a biased legal system, when a man dies by suicide, it's often dismissed as an isolated incident, even they die in dozens. But if a woman faces harm, it's treated as a national tragedy. Feminist organizations hold candlelight marches, demand government to change laws on single incident, while some fringe elements resort to vandalism and destruction of public property. Meanwhile, the media and vested interests often amplify their own additional narrative with continuous and sensationalized coverage.

THEY DID NOT TAKE THEIR OWN LIVES, BUT THEY WERE MURDERED BY THE LEGAL TERRORISM, THE INDIAN GOVERNMENT AND THE LAW MAKERS WHO FAILED THEM.

Minor Actors of Legal terrorism

Feminist Groups, NGOs

The advancement of women's rights has been a significant achievement of modern societies, with various feminist groups, NGOs, women's organizations, and government ministries working tirelessly to promote gender equality and protect women from abuse and discrimination. Laws such as Section 498A of the Indian Penal Code (IPC) and the Protection of Women from Domestic Violence Act (PWDVA) have been enacted to safeguard women's rights and provide recourse against domestic violence and harassment. However, concerns have been raised about the potential misuse of these laws, leading to what some refer to as "legal terrorism."

Legal Provisions and Their Intent

Section 498A, introduced in 1983, aims to protect women from cruelty by husbands or their families, with punishments including imprisonment and fines. The PWDVA (2005) provides civil remedies like protection orders, maintenance, and residence rights to women facing domestic violence. Divorce and maintenance laws under various personal laws (Hindu Marriage Act, Muslim Personal Law, etc.) allow women to seek financial support post-separation, while child custody laws prioritize the child's welfare, often favouring mothers, especially for younger children.

These laws were enacted to address genuine grievances of women in a historically patriarchal society where dowry harassment, domestic violence, and economic dependence were rampant. However, critics argue that their broad language and non-bailable, cognizable nature (in the case of 498A) make them prone to misuse, enabling women to weaponize legal processes against husbands for ulterior motives like securing divorce, extracting money, or settling personal scores.

Misuse: Motives and Patterns

Various Studies claim that many women, particularly in urban areas (now-days it's a trend), misuse these laws when seeking divorce, financial maintenance, or to deflect scrutiny from extramarital affairs. Common scenarios include:

- **Divorce and Maintenance**: When a marriage sours, women may file 498A or PWDVA cases to pressure husbands into agreeing to favourable divorce settlements, including high maintenance payments. The threat of criminal charges or prolonged litigation often coerces men into compliance.

- **Extramarital Affairs**: If a husband discovers an affair, women may pre-emptively file cases to shift blame, portraying themselves as victims of cruelty or violence. This deflects attention from their actions and strengthens their legal position in divorce or custody battles.

- **Child Custody and Visitation**: By alleging cruelty or violence, women can secure favourable custody rulings, as courts prioritize the child's safety. Men may also be denied visitation rights if portrayed as threats, leaving them emotionally and financially drained.

- **Financial Extortion**: The promise of withdrawing cases in exchange for large settlements is a frequent accusation. Men, fearing social stigma, job loss, or jail time, may pay substantial sums to avoid protracted legal battles.

Role of Feminist Groups, NGOs, and Ministries

Critics argue that feminist organizations, women's NGOs, and government bodies, including women's commissions and ministries, play a significant role in enabling or encouraging such misuse, either directly or indirectly. Their alleged contributions include:

Uncritical Support for Women's Claims:

Feminist groups and NGOs often adopt a "believe all women" stance, providing legal, emotional, and financial support without thoroughly verifying allegations. This can embolden women to file exaggerated or false complaints, knowing they will face little scrutiny.

Women's cells and counselling centres, often funded by NGOs or government bodies, may guide women to file cases under 498A or PWDVA as a first resort, even in disputes that could be resolved through mediation.

Feminist groups, NGOs, and women's organizations play a crucial role in raising awareness about women's rights, providing support to victims of abuse, and advocating for policy changes. They offer legal aid, counselling, and rehabilitation services to women in need. However, critics argue that some of these groups may, inadvertently or otherwise, encourage the misuse of laws intended to protect women.

For instance, in cases where a woman seeks divorce and maintenance, or when she is accused of infidelity, some organizations might advise her to use legal provisions like 498A IPC or PWDVA as bargaining tools. This can lead to false or exaggerated cases being filed against husbands, causing them significant emotional, reputational, and financial distress. Such misuse not only harms the accused but also undermines the credibility of genuine victims and the legal system as a whole.

Legal Aid and Advocacy:

Many NGOs offer free legal aid to women, making it easier to initiate cases without personal financial risk. While intended to help genuinely abused women, this can also facilitate frivolous or vindictive complaints.

Feminist advocates often lobby for stricter laws and faster judicial processes, which critics argue reduces due diligence, leading to hasty arrests or biased rulings against men.

Media and Social Pressure:

Feminist narratives in media, amplified by Women NGOs, Feminists and Women Ministries often portray women as perpetual victims and men as oppressors. This creates a social climate where men's grievances are dismissed, and women's allegations are presumed true, pressuring courts to rule in their favour.

Public campaigns by women's groups rarely acknowledge misuse, framing any critique of these laws as patriarchal backlash, which stifles balanced discourse.

Government and Policy Support:

Ministries like the Ministry of Women and Child Development and bodies like the National Commission for Women (NCW) are mandated to protect women's rights. However, critics argue they often act as enablers by uncritically backing women's complaints or pushing for policies that prioritize women's interests over fairness.

For instance, the NCW's role in fast-tracking 498A cases has been criticized for bypassing due process, leading to automatic arrests of husbands and their families, including elderly parents or siblings, without evidence.

Government ministries, such as the Ministry of Women and Child Development, are responsible for promoting the welfare and rights of women. They implement policies, programs, and laws aimed at empowering women and protecting them from violence and discrimination. However, these ministries may not always have robust mechanisms to prevent the misuse of these laws.

The Concept of "Legal Terrorism"

The term "legal terrorism" was popularized by men's rights activists and even referenced by the Supreme Court of India in cases like Sushil Kumar Sharma v.

Union of India (2005), where the court acknowledged the potential for 498A's misuse to harass husbands. The characteristics of this phenomenon include:

Psychological and Financial Harassment: Prolonged litigation, social stigma, and financial burdens (legal fees, maintenance) devastate men and their families.

Weaponization of the Legal System: The non-bail-able nature of 498A and the broad scope of PWDVA allow women to wield these laws as tools of coercion, with little immediate recourse for men.

Erosion of Trust in Institutions: Widespread perception of misuse undermines faith in the judiciary and law enforcement, as men feel targeted by a system that appears biased.

Data on misuse is sparse, but a 2011 study by the Centre for Social Research found that around 10-15% of 498A cases in urban areas might involve exaggerated or false claims, though this is not definitive. Courts have also noted rising instances of frivolous cases, with acquittal rates in 498A cases often exceeding 80%, suggesting weak evidence in many complaints.

The term "legal terrorism" refers to the misuse of legal provisions to harass, control, or dominate someone. In the context of gender laws, it can manifest as false cases filed under 498A IPC, PWDVA, or other divorce and maintenance laws. Husbands and their families may face arrest, prolonged legal battles, and demands for large sums as maintenance or settlements. Even when the accusations are eventually proven false, the damage to the accused's life and reputation can be irreversible.

Moreover, the threat of such cases can be used to force husbands to concede to demands related to child custody or visitation rights. This can result in children being used as bargaining chips, which is detrimental to their well-being and emotional development.

Conclusion

While laws like 498A and PWDVA were designed to protect women, their alleged misuse, facilitated by feminist groups, NGOs, and governmental bodies, has sparked accusations of "legal terrorism." These groups, through legal aid, advocacy, and uncritical support, are seen by critics as enabling women to harass husbands for financial or personal gain, particularly in disputes over divorce, maintenance, or custody. However, the extent of misuse remains debated, and feminist organizations argue that such claims are overblown to discredit women's protections. Balancing the need to safeguard women with the prevention of legal abuse is crucial to ensure justice for all parties. A nuanced approach, combining judicial reforms, mediation, and open dialogue, is essential to address these complex issues without undermining the fight for gender equality.

Lawyers

In India, the legal system is often seen as a tool for justice, but it can also be manipulated to serve unjust ends. Laws like **Section 498A** of the Indian Penal Code (IPC), the **Protection of Women from Domestic Violence Act (PWDVA)**, maintenance laws, child custody regulations, and laws addressing rape have been instrumental in protecting women's rights. However, the misuse of these laws has raised significant concerns over the role of lawyers in perpetuating false cases. Here we explore how lawyers contribute to this phenomenon, they are the minor actors in this Legal terrorism, the lack of accountability in the legal profession, and suggests reforms for the Advocates Act to enhance integrity and professionalism among legal practitioners.

A key issue in this misuse is the **lack of accountability among legal practitioners**. Some lawyers, in pursuit of monetary gain or under the guise of women's empowerment, may advise clients—especially women—to file **false or exaggerated complaints**. In such cases, women are encouraged to file multiple cases under various provisions, often simultaneously, creating a web of legal complications for the accused

Lawyers and False Cases

This is enabled by several troubling trends:

- **Lawyers exploit the system** by dragging cases for years, demanding fees on every court appearance.
- Innocent men, even with proof of their innocence, often face **delayed justice** as lawyers for the opposing side use every legal trick to prolong litigation.
- **Men's lawyers too are not always fair**, sometimes refusing to attend hearings, showing apathy, or prioritizing high-paying clients—leaving men defenceless and vulnerable.
- Once a false case is filed, even if it's later disproved, **lawyers rarely face any consequences**. There is no mechanism to evaluate or penalize unethical conduct in advising or supporting malicious litigation.

Advising and Supporting Women

Lawyers often act as advisors and advocates for women in cases of alleged violence, dowry demands, and domestic abuse. While their role in supporting victims is valuable, it is essential to recognize instances where legal counsel may lead to the filing of false cases. Lawyers may encourage women to file complaints or lawsuits that are exaggerated or unfounded, motivated by the potential for financial gain or as part of larger societal trends favouring women in legal contexts.

Misuse of Legal Provisions

Some provisions, notably **Section 498A IPC** and maintenance laws, have been criticized for misuse. They allow women to file complaints against their husbands and in-laws for cruelty or dowry demands, often leading to arrests and severe social stigma for the accused, irrespective of the truth. Lawyers may exploit the lack of accountability and oversight in the legal system, cumulatively contributing to a rising number of false cases that financially and emotionally drain innocent men.

Harassment and Exploitation of Men

Men, often targeted by these laws, face harassment in various forms. Lawyers may not provide adequate representation, intentionally dragging cases and scheduling delays while charging fees for every hearing. This tactic not only serves to exploit the accused financially but also extends the psychological torment of protracted legal battles. Such behaviour diminishes the integrity of the legal profession and undermines faith in the judicial system.

Harassment Faced by Innocent Men

For men wrongly accused, the consequences are grave:

- **Arrests without investigation**, especially in dowry cases.
- **Loss of reputation, job, and social standing**.
- Years of mental stress, legal expenses, and in many cases, being **denied access to their children** in custody battles.
- Lack of support from society due to the stigma of being accused, even before trial or verdict.

Accountability Deficiencies

The accountability of lawyers in India is alarmingly low. There exists a pervasive culture of impunity within the legal profession, allowing unethical practices to thrive. This lack of regulation means:

- **Misrepresentation of Cases**: Lawyers may misrepresent the likelihood of case outcomes to clients, particularly when financial incentives are involved.
- **Inadequate Defence**: The legal representatives may deliberately neglect their duty to effectively defend clients, especially men who are falsely accused.
- **Fee Exploitation**: Charging exorbitant fees for services that may not be rendered appropriately adds to the systemic problem of

accountability. Introduce a minimum standard of payment and require lawyers to provide written acknowledgment of payments and agreed-upon tasks. Many lawyers, after receiving payment, fail to attend court hearings or offer services, and when clients question them, they are advised to seek a new lawyer. This practice needs to be addressed for the sake of fairness and accountability.

Suggested Reforms for the Advocates Act

The Advocates Act 1961 governs the legal profession in India, but it requires urgent reforms to promote accountability and ethical practices. Suggested reforms include:

1. **Establishment of a Regulatory Body**: A dedicated regulatory authority should be instituted to oversee lawyer conduct, ensuring adherence to ethical standards.
2. **Mandatory Training and Certification**: Implementing compulsory training programs focused on ethical practices, case handling, and appropriate client counselling can equip lawyers to understand the consequences of false allegations.
3. **Streamlining Complaints Mechanism**: A streamlined, accessible complaints mechanism should be in place for clients to report lawyer

misconduct. Swift action on these complaints is essential to uphold trust in the legal system.

4. **Transparency in Fees**: Introducing guidelines that mandate transparency in fee structures can prevent exploitation of clients and promote fair practices.

5. **Timely Disposition of Cases**: Strengthening judicial procedures to ensure timely hearings can reduce the chances of misuse of laws by discouraging protracted litigation.

6. **Accountability Measures**: Implementing consequences for lawyers who are found guilty of unethical practices, including suspension or disbarment, can deter misconduct.

7. **Complaint to Bar Council**: Complaints to the Bar Council should be free of charge. Currently, a fee of Rs. 3000 is charged for filing any complaint, along with the requirement to submit multiple copies of the complaint. Any fees should only be paid by the lawyer or advocate if they are found guilty.

8. **Lawyers Legal Fees and Service**: Lawyer Fees should be subject to Income Tax regulations. Additionally, financial incentives or tax breaks should be provided for advocates who offer a portion of their services for free. The lawyer should sign the Terms of Service (TOS) when receiving the Vakalathnama. The TOS should clearly outline the fees, services offered, and the lawyer's responsibilities, including attending all court dates, drafting petitions, IAs, memos, pleadings, and handling all aspects of the case until its conclusion,

including providing the final copy of the judgment/order. While many lawyers prefer a one-time payment, it's important to offer clients the option to pay in two or three instalments, as many may not be able to pay the full amount upfront. Additionally, some lawyers drag out cases and demand payment for each court appearance; this practice should be discontinued.

9. **Complaint against Lawyer**: There should be a comprehensive list of lawyers available online through the district or state level Bar Council websites, and the option to file complaints against such lawyers should also be made available online for public access.

   - **Strict disciplinary action** against lawyers proven to be advising or facilitating false cases, including suspension or disbarment.
   - **Mandatory audit or review** of cases dismissed as false, with inquiry into the conduct of the representing lawycrs.
   - **Performance tracking system** for advocates—tracking attendance, client feedback, case timelines, and success rates.
   - **Stronger role for Bar Councils** to act proactively, not just in response to complaints.
   - **Introduction of a grievance redressal mechanism** for litigants against

lawyers, especially when clients face negligence or exploitation.

Conclusion

The responsibility of lawyers in India extends beyond mere representation to a pivotal role in upholding justice. When they advise clients to pursue false cases, the consequences ripple through society, affecting innocent lives and eroding trust in the legal system. The current lack of accountability for legal practitioners exacerbates this issue. By implementing substantive reforms to the Advocates Act, we can foster a legal environment that prioritizes integrity, fairness, and justice for all, ensuring that the law serves its intended purpose without being manipulated for personal gain.

Judges

The Role of Judges in Enabling Gender-Biased Injustice

India's family courts were established with the noble intent of resolving domestic disputes with compassion, speed, and fairness. However, over the years, a growing number of litigants—especially men—have begun to voice concerns that these courts have strayed from the principles of justice and equality. What has emerged is a form of **"legal terrorism,"** wherein judicial bias, unchecked perjury, and discriminatory judgments have turned the legal system into a tool of harassment rather than resolution.

The Indian judiciary, especially family courts, is ostensibly designed to provide equitable dispute resolution for familial issues, including maintenance, custody, and domestic violence cases. However, the rise of what has been termed legal terrorism, the phenomenon where provisions of law are manipulated to intimidate or exploit one party — has raised significant concerns regarding the role of judges in these courts. This essay critically analyses how Indian family court judges may inadvertently promote legal terrorism by favouring women in cases of maintenance and child custody, often overlooking falsehoods in claims and allowing a culture where the rights of men and fathers are marginalized.

Judicial Bias in Favour of Women

One of the most serious allegations against Indian family court judges is that they consistently favour women, regardless of the merits of the case. In disputes involving maintenance, domestic violence, and child custody, judges often assume women to be victims and men as oppressors. This presumption goes against the principle of natural justice and the idea that every person is innocent until proven guilty.

In maintenance cases under Section 125 CrPC, Hindu Marriage Act (HMA), and other personal laws, men are routinely ordered to pay heavy amounts—even when:

The woman is well-qualified or more educated than the husband.

She is earning a better income or is deliberately choosing to remain unemployed.

The husband is under financial stress or supporting aged parents.

Such rulings promote dependency rather than empowerment, and reward non-working, capable women at the cost of men's livelihood.

Gender-Specific Judgments

It is observed that family court judges frequently demonstrate a pattern of bias that leans in favour of women. This bias is particularly evident in:

- Maintenance Awards: Under Section 125 of the Code of Criminal Procedure (CrPC) and the Hindu Marriage Act (HMA), courts award maintenance primarily to women, irrespective of their financial standing. Judgments have often favoured women even when they earn more than their male counterparts or possess higher education credentials.

- Child Custody: Judges tend to grant custody to mothers without adequately considering the father's rights or the best interests of the child. The persistent notion that mothers inherently provide better care leads to skewed judgments, side-lining fathers who also wish to partake in their children's lives.

Ignoring Falsehoods and Perjury

In many cases, women file multiple cases—ranging from domestic violence to dowry harassment to child custody—all based on the same or exaggerated set of facts. Family court judges rarely question the veracity of these claims. Worse still, even when it is proven that the woman lied under oath, judges refuse to initiate perjury proceedings under Section 340 CrPC.

The standard excuse? That pursuing perjury would "open the floodgates" and overburden the courts. But this reasoning effectively gives women a license to lie, secure in the knowledge that there will be no consequences. It also undermines the credibility of the entire justice system.

One of the critical causes of **legal terrorism** in family courts is the failure to address perjury. Judges often dismiss applications for perjury under Section 340 of the CrPC, cautioning that such actions might "open floodgates" of litigation. This approach has several repercussions:

- Undermining Truth and Justice: By ignoring clear instances of falsehoods in claims, judges foster an environment where deceit can thrive without consequences. This negligence allows unscrupulous individuals to manipulate the legal system for personal gain.

- Victimization of Innocent Parties: Men and fathers become easy victims in this scenario. Without recourse to challenge false allegations effectively, they are left to navigate a complicated legal system that can drag on for years, often damaging their livelihoods and mental health.

Delays and the Impact on Fathers

In child custody matters, Indian courts overwhelmingly award custody to the mother, often treating the father as a mere visitor in the life of his own child. Visitation rights, when granted, are limited, delayed, and poorly enforced. Fathers may wait for years or even decades to gain basic access, and during this time, courts do little to ensure that the mother complies with visitation orders.

Ironically, when the child grows up and questions the father's absence, the same system that denied access now asks the father, "Why didn't you visit?" This circular blame not only punishes the father but alienates the child and fractures the family bond permanently.

The long delays in family court proceedings represent a significant barrier to justice for fathers. Many fathers wait decades for even brief visitation rights, only to be questioned later about their absence in the child's life. The systemic issues include:

- Protraction of Visitation Rights: Delays in granting fathers visitation rights contribute to estrangement from their children, which can lead to further distress and complicate the parent-child relationship.

- Judicial Disregard for Men's Rights: When judges disproportionately uphold the rights of women while neglecting those of men, it undermines the essence of equality before the law as enshrined in the Indian Constitution. The perception that fathers are inherently less deserving of custody or visitation rights exacerbates societal biases.

Consequences of a Gender-Biased Legal System

The promotion of legal terrorism through biased judicial behaviour has far-reaching consequences:

- **Erosion of Trust**: Men and fathers may lose faith in the legal system, feeling that their rights are not protected or respected. This distrust undermines the legitimacy of family courts as institutions intended to deliver justice.
- **Escalation of Conflicts**: When one party experiences continuous legal advantages, it can escalate familial conflicts and lead to ongoing legal battles, making reconciliation between parties increasingly difficult.

- **Financial Burden**: Unreasonably high maintenance awards can strain men's finances, forcing them to contribute heavily to their estranged spouses while simultaneously battling for the right to see their children.

The phenomenon of *legal terrorism* in family courts highlights significant flaws in the judicial approach toward gender-based disputes in India. While family courts exist to provide justice and protection, the inherent biases exhibited by judges can lead to the victimization of men and fathers, perpetuating a cycle of legal exploitation. Addressing these issues through systemic reforms, including enhanced judicial training and accountability measures, is essential to restore balance and uphold the ideals of justice within the family law system. Only with equitable treatment can the legal arena serve its purpose of safeguarding the rights and responsibilities of all individuals within a family.

Implementing rigorous training programs for family court judges focused on gender-neutral application of laws can mitigate biases. Judges must understand the implications of their awards on both parties.

Formulating clear guidelines that dictate how judges should assess maintenance and custody cases, including a thorough consideration of both parents' financial situations and contributions to the family.

Major Actors of the Legal Terrorism

Supreme Court of India

In recent years, the Indian judicial system, particularly the Supreme Court, has increasingly acknowledged the misuse of laws intended for the protection of women. Notably, terms like "legal terrorism" have been used by the apex court to describe the blatant misuse of certain provisions such as Section 498A of the Indian Penal Code (IPC), the Protection of Women from Domestic Violence Act (PWDVA), and occasionally in the context of false allegations under POCSO and rape laws. Despite these observations, a significant concern raised by men's rights activists and legal analysts is the absence of punitive action against those who misuse such laws, leading to what is being called a silent endorsement of legal misuse — or "legal terrorism."

The term "legal terrorism" has emerged in Indian legal discourse to describe the alleged misuse of laws, particularly those designed to protect women, to harass or intimidate men and their families. Critics argue that laws such as Section 498A of the Indian Penal Code (IPC), the Protection of Women from Domestic Violence Act (PWDVA), the Protection of Children from Sexual Offences Act (POCSO), and rape-related provisions are weaponized to settle personal scores, leading to prolonged harassment of innocent individuals. The Supreme Court of India, tasked with upholding justice, has occasionally acknowledged the misuse of these laws, even using the phrase "legal terrorism" in certain judgments. However, the claim that the Supreme Court exhibits a "soft corner" for women, allowing them to go unpunished while enabling legal terrorism, warrants a nuanced examination of judicial trends, legal frameworks, and societal dynamics.

The Context of "Legal Terrorism"

The term "legal terrorism" gained prominence following the Supreme Court's observations in cases involving Section 498A, which addresses cruelty by a husband or his relatives toward a married woman. In *Sushil Kumar Sharma v. Union of India* (2005), the Court noted that the misuse of Section 498A could unleash "legal terrorism," as exaggerated or false complaints sometimes led to the harassment of innocent men and their families. The Court highlighted how such misuse undermined the law's original intent to protect women from dowry-related abuse and domestic cruelty. Similarly, in *Preeti Gupta v. State of Jharkhand* (2010), the Court cautioned against the *"tendency to implicate the entire family"* in 498A cases, urging lower courts to scrutinize complaints for veracity.

These observations reflect a judicial acknowledgment of systemic issues. Section 498A, for instance, is a non-bailable and cognizable offense, meaning arrests can be made without a warrant, often leading to immediate detention of the accused. Critics argue that this provision, combined with societal biases favoring women's complaints in matrimonial disputes, creates fertile ground for misuse. The low conviction rate under Section 498A—reportedly around 15% as per National Crime Records Bureau (**NCRB**) data—further fuels the narrative that many cases are baseless or filed with ulterior motives.

The Origin and Purpose of Protective Laws

Laws like Section 498A IPC and PWDVA were enacted with the noble intent of protecting women from dowry-related violence, domestic abuse, and sexual crimes — a much-needed response to centuries of patriarchal oppression. These laws were designed to provide speedy relief and support to genuine victims, often through immediate arrests, restraining orders, and the presumption of guilt in sensitive cases.

However, over time, concerns began to surface regarding the potential for misuse. The Supreme Court itself, in *Sushil Kumar Sharma vs Union of India* (2005), noted that "the provision is being used as a weapon rather than a shield by disgruntled wives." In *Arnesh Kumar vs State of Bihar* (2014), the court took cognizance of arbitrary arrests under Section 498A and issued guidelines to prevent its misuse. Still, no systemic penalties were introduced for those who were proven to have lodged false complaints.

Acquittals Without Penalties: A Systemic Issue?

The essay's central contention is that the Supreme Court frequently acquits men and their families in cases of alleged misuse but rarely penalizes women who file false complaints. Historical data partially supports this claim. While the Supreme Court and lower courts have quashed numerous frivolous cases under Section 498A, PWDVA, POCSO, or rape laws, instances of women being prosecuted for perjury or malicious prosecution are rare. For example, in *Kaur v. State* (2017), the Court acquitted the accused in a 498A case, noting the complaint's lack of evidence, but did not initiate action against the complainant. Similarly, in *Arnesh Kumar v. State of Bihar* (2014), the Court issued guidelines to prevent automatic arrests in 498A cases, citing misuse, but stopped short of mandating penalties for false complaints.

This trend raises questions about judicial accountability. Under Section 182 of the IPC, giving false information to cause injury is punishable, yet prosecutions under this provision in the context of matrimonial or sexual offense laws are seldom pursued. The absence of penalties may stem from several factors. First, proving mala fide intent in filing a complaint is challenging, as courts prioritize protecting genuine victims over deterring potential misuse. Second, judicial restraint may reflect a concern that penalizing women could discourage legitimate complaints, especially in a society where patriarchal structures still impede access to justice for many women. Third, the overburdened judiciary often prioritizes resolving primary disputes over initiating secondary prosecutions for perjury.

Allegations of a "Soft Corner" for Women

The claim that the Supreme Court has a "soft corner" for women, allowing them to go "scot-free," oversimplifies a complex issue. India's legal framework for protecting women was developed in response to systemic gender-based violence, including dowry deaths, domestic abuse, and sexual offenses. Laws like Section 498A and PWDVA were enacted to address historical imbalances, where women faced significant barriers in seeking redress. The judiciary, aware of this context, often adopts a cautious approach to avoid undermining these protections. For instance, in *State of Haryana vs. Bhajan Lal* (1992), the Court emphasized the need to balance the prevention of misuse with the protection of genuine victims.

However, this cautious approach can sometimes appear as leniency. The lack of proactive measures to penalize false complaints contrasts with the Court's willingness to issue guidelines curbing misuse, such as in *Arnesh Kumar or Rajesh Sharma vs. State* (2017), where family welfare committees were proposed to vet 498A complaints (later struck down). Critics argue that this asymmetry—strict scrutiny of complaints but reluctance to punish false accusers—creates a perception of bias. The absence of notable Supreme Court cases where women face consequences for misuse under 498A, PWDVA, or POCSO reinforces this view.

The Impact on Innocent Men and Families

Men falsely accused under these laws often undergo years of trial, social ostracization, career setbacks, emotional trauma, and financial ruin. Entire families, including elderly parents and even children, have been implicated in such cases, only to be acquitted after decades of legal battle. While the courts have shown sympathy in such situations, acquittals alone offer no restitution for the damage suffered. The complainants, even if found to have intentionally filed false cases, often walk away without consequences.

This pattern has led to growing frustration among affected men and advocacy groups who argue that the judiciary, while recognizing misuse, has failed to implement accountability. The term "legal terrorism" — used by the judiciary itself — underscores the gravity of this misuse. But if the court recognizes this form of terror and fails to act against its perpetrators, it raises uncomfortable questions about judicial impartiality.

Gender Bias or Societal Sensitivity?

Critics argue that the Supreme Court's reluctance to penalize women who misuse protective laws may stem from an over-cautious approach rooted in social sensitivity. India continues to grapple with widespread gender-based violence, and courts may fear that penalizing women for false allegations could discourage genuine victims from coming forward. While this concern is not unfounded, it cannot justify allowing the judicial system to be weaponized without consequences.

There is also a broader issue of institutional and societal bias. While women's protection is rightly prioritized, the notion that men cannot be victims — or that women cannot be aggressors — reinforces damaging stereotypes. Justice must be gender-neutral, and the principle of "innocent until proven guilty" should not be selectively applied.

Does the Supreme Court Enable Legal Terrorism?

The assertion that the Supreme Court is "behind legal terrorism" is contentious and requires scrutiny. The Court's role is to interpret and uphold the law, not to create it. The framework of laws like Section 498A or PWDVA, which critics label as prone to misuse, is a product of legislative intent, not judicial design. The Court has, in fact, taken steps to mitigate misuse, such as issuing guidelines to prevent automatic arrests and urging lower courts to exercise caution.

However, its reluctance to penalize false complainants or push for legislative reforms may contribute to the perception of enabling legal terrorism indirectly.

Moreover, the judiciary operates within a broader societal context. Gender dynamics in India, where women remain vulnerable to violence and discrimination, influence judicial priorities. The Court's hesitance to penalize women may reflect a fear of chilling legitimate complaints, but this approach risks alienating men who face harassment through false cases. A balanced solution would require legislative reforms to strengthen safeguards against misuse—such as mandatory preliminary inquiries or stricter penalties for perjury—while preserving protections for genuine victims.

The Supreme Court's acknowledgment of "legal terrorism" highlights a real issue: the misuse of laws like Section 498A, PWDVA, POCSO, and rape provisions can cause significant harm to innocent men and their families. While the Court has acquitted many wrongfully accused individuals, its failure to consistently penalize those who misuse these laws fuels perceptions of bias and leniency toward women. However, labelling the Supreme Court as "behind legal terrorism" overlooks the complexities of India's legal and social landscape. The judiciary operates within the constraints of existing laws and societal pressures, striving to balance the protection of vulnerable women with the prevention of harassment through frivolous complaints. To address the issue of legal terrorism effectively, both judicial and legislative reforms are needed—ones that deter misuse without undermining the fight against gender-based violence. Only through such measures can the Indian legal system achieve true equity and justice for all.

Is the Supreme Court Complicit?

It would not be an overstatement to say the Supreme Court of India is behind legal terrorism. However, its consistent failure to enforce accountability for the misuse of protective laws does create a perception of judicial leniency — or a "soft corner" — towards women complainants, irrespective of the veracity of their claims. This not only undermines the credibility of genuine victims but also corrodes public trust in the legal system.

It is the responsibility of the Supreme Court of India to address deficiencies and loopholes in the legal system by issuing directives to subordinate courts and judges and recommending amendments to the government to curb misuse. Failure to do so raises concerns that the Court may be inadvertently contributing to the perpetuation of legal terrorism.

To restore balance, the judiciary must evolve beyond verbal acknowledgment. Mechanisms must be established to identify malicious litigants and hold them accountable through fines, public apologies, or criminal charges for perjury. Legal protection must never become a tool of persecution, and justice must serve all — not just one gender.

Politicians and Ministers.

How Indian Politicians Promote One-Sided Laws Favoring Women

In the pursuit of gender equality, Indian lawmakers have increasingly crafted legislation aimed at protecting women from violence, harassment, and discrimination. While the intent behind these laws is noble, the execution has often been lopsided, creating a framework that disproportionately favors women while ignoring the plight of men. This phenomenon, often termed "legal terrorism," refers to the misuse of gender-specific laws to harass, intimidate, or extort men, with little to no recourse for male victims. Indian politicians, driven by the allure of women as a vote bank and influenced by feminist organizations, have contributed to this imbalance by enacting and promoting one-sided laws that assume women are always victims, while dismissing the reality of men facing harassment, false accusations, and even violence at the hands of women.

In the democratic fabric of any nation, laws are designed to provide justice, protect citizens, and ensure equality before the law. However, in India, a growing number of voices are raising concerns over what they perceive as "legal terrorism"—a term used to describe the misuse of certain gender-specific laws, particularly those favouring women, to harass and victimise men. The political class, influenced by vote-bank politics and powerful feminist lobbies, has been accused of promoting legal asymmetry that not only undermines justice but also erodes the fundamental principle of equality.

The Rise of Gender-Biased Laws in India

India's legal framework includes several laws designed to protect women, such as Section 498A of the Indian Penal Code (dowry harassment), the Protection of Women from Domestic Violence Act, 2005, and various provisions under the Sexual Harassment of Women at Workplace Act, 2013. These laws were introduced to address genuine issues like dowry deaths, domestic abuse, and workplace harassment. However, their implementation has revealed significant flaws. For instance, Section 498A, which addresses cruelty by husbands and their families, is often misused to settle personal scores, extract financial settlements, or harass men and their families. The law's non-bailable and cognizable nature means that arrests can be made without investigation, leading to countless cases where innocent men and their families are dragged into legal battles based on false or exaggerated claims.

Similarly, the Domestic Violence Act, while progressive in intent, defines "domestic violence" in a way that only women can be victims, ignoring the possibility of men facing emotional, physical, or financial abuse in relationships. The absence of gender-neutral provisions ensures that men have no legal avenue to seek redress, even when they are victims of violence or harassment. This one-sided approach is further exacerbated by laws like the Maintenance Act, which almost always favour women in financial disputes, regardless of the circumstances.

Gender-Specific Laws and the Problem of Misuse

India has several laws meant to protect women from abuse and violence, such as Section 498A of the Indian Penal Code (dealing with cruelty by husband or his relatives), the Protection of Women from Domestic Violence Act, 2005, and various provisions under sexual harassment and rape laws. While these laws were enacted with the noble intent of safeguarding women against patriarchal oppression and domestic violence, there is growing evidence and judicial acknowledgment of their misuse.

For instance, the Supreme Court of India in *Rajesh Sharma vs. State of U.P.* (2017) noted that Section 498A was being increasingly used as a "weapon rather than a shield" by some women to harass their husbands and in-laws. In many such cases, men are arrested without preliminary inquiry, families are harassed, and reputations are destroyed—often irreparably—even when the accusations are later found to be false or exaggerated.

The Political Motivation: Women as a Vote Bank

The root of this legal imbalance lies in the political motivations of Indian lawmakers. Women constitute nearly half of India's electorate, making them a critical vote bank. Politicians, eager to appeal to this demographic, champion women-centric laws as a means of showcasing their commitment to gender justice. This strategy is often amplified by feminist organizations, non-governmental organizations (NGOs), and bodies like the National Commission for Women (NCW) and the Ministry of Women and Child Development (WCD), which lobby for laws that exclusively protect women.

While these organizations play an important role in advocating for women's rights, their refusal to acknowledge the misuse of laws or the victimization of men has created a skewed narrative. For instance, feminist groups often argue that false cases are negligible, despite evidence suggesting otherwise. A 2010 study by the Delhi High Court noted that a significant number of cases under Section 498A were filed with malicious intent, yet no amendments have been made to curb misuse. Similarly, the NCW and WCD have consistently opposed gender-neutral laws, claiming they would dilute protections for women, even though such laws could ensure justice for all victims, regardless of gender.

The reluctance of Indian politicians to address the misuse of gender-specific laws stems from a politically motivated agenda. Women constitute a significant and growing vote bank. As a result, any demand to make laws gender-neutral or to include punishment clauses for misuse is often ignored or dismissed as "anti-women." Political parties, keen to portray themselves as champions of women's rights, avoid appearing unsympathetic to female voters, even at the cost of ignoring legitimate male grievances.

This vote-bank politics has led to a situation where male victims of domestic violence, harassment, or abuse have little or no legal recourse. Ironically, while women can file complaints under multiple laws for the same incident, men facing similar trauma are often told to "man up" or are ridiculed for expressing vulnerability.

The Reality of Male Victimization

Contrary to the narrative that only women are victims, there is growing evidence of men facing harassment, false accusations, and violence at the hands of women. According to data from the National Crime Records Bureau (NCRB), thousands of men are arrested annually under Section 498A, with a significant percentage of cases later found to be baseless. Men's rights organizations, such as the MyNation Hope Foundation, have documented cases where women have used legal provisions to blackmail husbands, extort money, or retaliate in personal disputes. In extreme cases, men have been driven to suicide due to the social stigma, financial ruin, and emotional trauma caused by false allegations.

Moreover, men who face physical or emotional abuse from their wives or partners have no legal recourse. The lack of laws recognizing male victims of domestic violence or harassment means that men are left to suffer in silence, with societal stereotypes further discouraging them from speaking out. In cases where women commit violent crimes against men—such as murder or assault—the legal system often treats these incidents with leniency, perpetuating the myth that women are incapable of being aggressors.

Men: The Invisible Victims

There are numerous documented cases where men have been harassed, blackmailed, or driven to suicide due to false accusations of domestic violence, dowry harassment, or rape. However, the absence of a dedicated commission for men or any specific laws to protect male victims reflects a glaring institutional apathy. According to the National Crime Records Bureau (NCRB), thousands of married men die by suicide every year due to family problems and abuse—but these statistics seldom prompt any legislative attention.

The demand for a National Commission for Men, gender-neutral laws, and penalties for misuse of legal provisions has been growing louder, but continues to be side-lined.

The Role of Feminists and NGOs in Perpetuating Legal Terrorism

Feminist organizations and NGOs play a significant role in shaping India's gender laws, but their approach has often been dogmatic. By framing every issue as a women's issue, these groups have created a binary where men are perpetually seen as oppressors and women as victims. This narrative ignores the complexity of human relationships and the potential for abuse to flow in any direction. When suggestions are made to introduce punishment clauses for false complaints or to make laws gender-neutral, feminist groups and bodies like the NCW vehemently oppose them, arguing that such measures would deter genuine victims from coming forward. However, this stance overlooks the harm caused by frivolous complaints, which clog the judicial system and undermine the credibility of real victims.

The refusal to address misuse is particularly glaring in the case of Section 498A. Despite repeated calls from the judiciary—including Supreme Court rulings urging safeguards to prevent abuse—no significant reforms have been implemented. Feminist organizations often cite low conviction rates as evidence that the law is not misused, ignoring the fact that many cases are settled out of court or withdrawn after causing irreparable harm to the accused.

Feminist organizations, NGOs, and institutions like the National Commission for Women (NCW) and the Ministry of Women and Child Development (WCD) have played a pivotal role in shaping women-centric laws. While their efforts to empower women(only Daughter-in-law) are laudable, their resistance to including safeguards against misuse in these laws has attracted criticism. Despite numerous recommendations by courts, legal experts, and men's rights activists to make these laws more balanced, such suggestions are routinely ignored.

These organizations often reject even the idea of penalties for filing false cases, arguing it will deter genuine victims from coming forward. However, this argument fails to acknowledge that justice must be blind—not biased. Protecting false complainants not only undermines the credibility of genuine victims but also clogs the judicial system, wasting time and resources.

According to the NCW and WCD, a man's mother and sisters are not considered 'women' under their mandate. These bodies primarily represent women as daughters-in-law, and when a man's mother or sisters seek support, they are often denied assistance on the grounds that they do not fall within the defined scope of protection. Women's ministries exhibit bias not just against men, but against their entire families as well.

The Consequences of One-Sided Laws

The consequences of this legal imbalance are far-reaching. For men, the misuse of laws like Section 498A leads to financial ruin, loss of reputation, and emotional trauma. Families are torn apart, with elderly parents and siblings often implicated in false cases. The judicial system, already overburdened, is further strained by frivolous complaints, delaying justice for genuine victims. Most importantly, the lack of gender-neutral laws perpetuates a culture of injustice, where one gender's suffering is ignored in the name of protecting another.

For society as a whole, these laws erode trust in the legal system. When men perceive that the law is biased against them, they become disillusioned, leading to a broader erosion of faith in institutions. Additionally, the narrative that only women can be victims undermines true gender equality, reinforcing stereotypes that portray men as inherently dominant and women as perpetually vulnerable.

The Path Forward: Toward Gender-Neutral Justice

To address the issue of legal terrorism, Indian politicians must move beyond populist measures and work toward a legal framework that is fair and inclusive. This could include:

- **Amending Existing Laws**: Introduce safeguards to prevent the misuse of laws like Section 498A, such as mandatory investigations before arrests and penalties for false complaints.
- **Gender-Neutral Legislation**: Revise laws like the Domestic Violence Act to recognize men as potential victims, ensuring that all forms of abuse are addressed, regardless of gender.
- **Judicial Reforms**: Establish fast-track courts to handle family disputes and false complaints, reducing the burden on the judicial system and ensuring swift justice.
- **Public Awareness**: Promote campaigns that challenge stereotypes about gender and victimization, encouraging men to speak out about their experiences.
- **Engaging Stakeholders**: Involve men's rights groups, feminist organizations, and civil society

in drafting balanced laws that protect all victims without being prone to misuse.

A Call for Legal Reform

Justice is not about favouring one gender over another; it is about ensuring fairness, equity, and due process for all citizens. Legal reforms must reflect the changing dynamics of society. Gender-specific laws may have been necessary at one point to correct historical wrongs, but clinging to them in a modern, evolving society without safeguards is unjust and dangerous.

Indian lawmakers must recognize that equality means protection and accountability for all, regardless of gender. A fair legal system should include:

- Gender-neutral domestic violence laws.
- Punishment clauses for filing false cases.
- A men's welfare ministry or commission.
- Awareness campaigns on male abuse and suicide.
- A balanced approach to family and matrimonial disputes.

Conclusion

Indian politicians, driven by electoral considerations and feminist lobbying, have created a legal landscape that disproportionately favours women, often at the expense of men. While laws aimed at protecting women are essential, their one-sided nature and susceptibility to misuse have given rise to a form of legal terrorism that victimizes men and undermines justice. By refusing to acknowledge male victimization or address the misuse of laws, politicians, feminist organizations, and bodies like the NCW and WCD perpetuate an unjust system that harms both men, his family and the credibility of the legal framework. True gender equality can only be achieved through balanced, gender-neutral laws that recognize the complexity of human relationships and ensure justice for all, regardless of gender. It is time for India's lawmakers to rise above vote-bank politics and work toward a legal system that is fair, inclusive, and free from the spectre of legal terrorism.

While women's safety and empowerment remain essential goals, they must not come at the cost of justice and fairness for men. The misuse of gender-biased laws has created a parallel form of injustice—where men are presumed guilty, denied legal remedies, and often destroyed by false accusations. It is time for Indian politicians to rise above vote-bank politics and enact reforms that truly serve the cause of justice. Equality before the law should not be a selective privilege—it must be a universal right.

Women-Centric, Gender-biased Laws in India

A Critical Analysis

Across the world, the rule of law is rooted in the fundamental principle that all individuals are equal in the eyes of the law. Laws are ideally designed to serve justice impartially, protect rights, and ensure fairness irrespective of gender, caste, class, or religion. However, in India, certain laws such as Section 498A of the Indian Penal Code (IPC), the Protection of Women from Domestic Violence Act (PWDVA), provisions for divorce and maintenance under various personal laws, and special provisions like those under the Rape Law and the Protection of Children from Sexual Offences (POCSO) Act appear to be heavily skewed in favour of women. This raises a critical question: Why are these laws not gender-neutral?

India, a nation celebrated for its diversity and constitutional commitment to equality, has enacted several laws aimed at protecting and empowering women. Laws such as Section 498A of the Indian Penal Code (IPC), the Protection of Women from Domestic Violence Act (PWDVA), divorce and maintenance provisions, rape laws, and the Protection of Children from Sexual Offences Act (POCSO) are often cited as women-centric. Critics argue that these laws disproportionately favour women, sometimes at the expense of fairness to men, and lack gender neutrality. This essay explores the reasons behind the women-centric nature of these laws, the resistance from women's NGOs, the Ministry of Women and Child Development, and feminists to make them gender-neutral, and the motivations of the Indian government in enacting such legislation.

Historical and Social Context of Women-Centric Laws

The genesis of women-centric laws in India lies in the country's patriarchal history and systemic gender inequalities. For centuries, women in India faced discrimination, violence, and marginalization in both public and private spheres. Dowry-related violence, domestic abuse, sexual assault, and unequal treatment in marriage and inheritance were rampant. In response, the Indian government, influenced by global feminist movements and domestic activism, introduced laws to address these injustices. For instance, Section 498A was enacted in 1983 to combat dowry harassment and cruelty by husbands and their families. Similarly, the PWDVA (2005) aimed to provide comprehensive protection to women from domestic violence, recognizing their vulnerability within the family structure.

These laws were designed to level the playing field in a society where women have historically been disadvantaged. The rationale was that women, due to their socio-economic dependence, lack of agency, and exposure to specific forms of violence, required targeted legal protections. Rape laws and POCSO, while primarily addressing sexual violence, also reflect this intent by focusing on women and children as primary victims, given the prevalence of gender-based violence against them.

Why Are These Laws Perceived as One-Sided?

Critics argue that laws like Section 498A, PWDVA, and maintenance provisions are prone to misuse due to their women-centric framing. Section 498A, for example, allows women to file complaints against their husbands and in-laws for cruelty, with non-bailable and cognizable offenses that can lead to immediate arrests. Reports suggest that false or exaggerated complaints are sometimes filed to settle personal scores or gain leverage in matrimonial disputes. Similarly, maintenance laws under Section 125 of the Code of Criminal Procedure and the Hindu Marriage Act often mandate financial support for women post-separation, with limited scrutiny of the husband's circumstances or the wife's earning potential.

Rape laws and POCSO, while critical for addressing sexual violence, are also criticized for their gender-specific language. For instance, under Indian law, only women can be victims of rape (Section 375 IPC), leaving male victims of sexual assault with limited legal recourse. This has fuelled perceptions that the legal framework is biased, ignoring men's vulnerabilities or potential victimization.

Concerns Regarding Gender Bias and Misuse

However, as Indian society evolves and women gain more social, economic, and political power, criticism has grown over the alleged one-sidedness of these laws. Men's rights activists, legal experts, and even some judicial pronouncements have raised concerns about the misuse of women-centric laws. For example, the Supreme Court of India has acknowledged that Section 498A has at times been misused as a tool for harassment and extortion rather than protection.

In cases of rape, divorce, and maintenance, critics argue that the law assumes women to always be victims and men as perpetrators — ignoring the complexities of modern relationships where abuse and injustice can occur irrespective of gender. The lack of legal recognition for male victims of domestic violence or false rape accusations is cited as a major flaw in India's pursuit of true equality under the law.

Resistance to Gender-Neutral Laws

The opposition to making these laws gender-neutral primarily comes from women's NGOs, feminist groups, and the Ministry of Women and Child Development. Several factors contribute to this stance:

Fear of Diluting Protections for Women: Feminist groups argue that gender-neutral laws could undermine the hard-won protections for women in a patriarchal society. They contend that women remain disproportionately affected by domestic violence, dowry harassment, and sexual assault due to power imbalances. Neutralizing these laws might weaken their effectiveness, as men, who often hold greater social and economic power, may exploit such provisions to counter-accuse women, thus discouraging genuine victims from coming forward.

Statistical Justification: Data from the National Crime Records Bureau (NCRB) consistently shows higher rates of violence against women compared to men. For instance, in 2021, over 4,28,000 cases of crimes against women were reported, including dowry deaths, domestic violence, and rape. Women's NGOs cite such statistics to argue that women-specific laws are necessary to address this reality. They view gender-neutral laws as a premature step in a society where women's safety remains a pressing concern.

Socio-Cultural Context: Feminist scholars emphasize that laws like 498A and PWDVA were crafted to counter deeply entrenched cultural practices, such as dowry and marital violence, which predominantly affect women. Neutralizing these laws could shift focus away from systemic gender issues, potentially trivializing the structural disadvantages women face.

Institutional Bias: The Ministry of Women and Child Development, tasked with advancing women's welfare, naturally prioritizes women's issues. Its mandate and funding are tied to women-centric policies, creating an institutional bias against gender-neutral reforms. Similarly, women's NGOs, often reliant on grants for women's empowerment programs, may resist changes that could redirect resources or attention to men's issues.

Why Opposition to Gender Neutrality?

Women's rights groups, feminist organizations, and ministries often fear and oppose making these laws gender-neutral, citing several reasons:

Asymmetrical Power Dynamics: They argue that gender neutrality can dilute the protective intent of the law, especially when women still face significant risks due to entrenched social and economic inequalities.

Statistical Justification: The majority of victims in cases like domestic violence and sexual assault are still overwhelmingly women. Hence, tailoring the law to protect the statistically more vulnerable group is seen as both pragmatic and necessary. But if given chance to men there will be reports of Crimes by Women more than crimes by Men, so that stop Feminists cry victim and claim funds.

Fear of Underreporting: Making laws gender-neutral might deter women from coming forward due to the fear of counter-litigation or shifting public sympathy.

Resource Constraints: There are concerns that if laws become gender-neutral without a corresponding increase in infrastructure (such as shelters, helplines, and legal aid for all genders), it could end up serving no one effectively and funds are divided equally that's the biggest fear of feminist when there are equal number or more Victim Men.

Government's Role in Enacting Gender biased Laws

The Government of India faces a challenging balancing act — between protecting vulnerable citizens and ensuring laws are fair to all. One reason for continuing women-centric laws is political and social pressure from powerful advocacy groups. Furthermore, legislative changes often require strong empirical data and societal readiness, both of which are still evolving in India.

However, there have been signs of progress. Courts have increasingly acknowledged the possibility of misuse and called for safeguards. Civil society too is becoming more vocal about men's rights and the need for legal parity.

The Indian government's inclination toward women-centric laws can be attributed to several factors:

Political Considerations: Women constitute nearly half of India's electorate, and addressing their concerns is politically advantageous. Governments, regardless of party, often prioritize women's safety and empowerment to appeal to this demographic. High-profile cases of violence against women, such as the 2012 Nirbhaya case, have further pressured lawmakers to strengthen women-specific legislation.

International Obligations: India is a signatory to international conventions like the Convention on the Elimination of All Forms of Discrimination Against Women (CEDAW), which mandates affirmative action to protect women's rights. Women-centric laws align with these global commitments, enhancing India's standing in international forums.

Judicial Influence: The Indian judiciary has played a significant role in shaping women-centric laws through landmark judgments. For instance, the *Vishaka Guidelines* (1997) laid the foundation for laws on workplace sexual harassment, emphasizing women's vulnerability. Courts often interpret laws in ways that prioritize women's protection, reinforcing the government's approach.

Social Advocacy: Women's movements and feminist activism have been instrumental in pushing for legal reforms. From the anti-dowry campaigns of the 1980s to the **#MeToo** movement (Lately exposed as Money making scheme), sustained advocacy has compelled the government to enact and maintain women-centric laws.

The Case for Gender Neutrality

Despite the rationale for women-centric laws, the demand for gender neutrality is gaining traction. Men's rights groups and civil society organizations argue that laws should reflect contemporary realities, where men can also be victims of domestic violence, false accusations, or sexual assault. For instance, studies like the 2014 Save Indian Family Foundation survey claimed that men face significant emotional and financial abuse in marriages, often exacerbated by biased laws. Gender-neutral laws could ensure fairness, reduce misuse, and promote equality in its truest sense.

Moreover, gender neutrality aligns with constitutional principles of equality under Article 14 and non-discrimination under Article 15. Critics of women-centric laws argue that their one-sided nature perpetuates stereotypes—portraying women as perpetual victims and men as inherent aggressors—thus undermining the broader goal of gender equality.

Conclusion

India's gender-specific laws were born out of a genuine need to protect women from centuries of oppression. However, the time has come to critically assess these laws in the context of changing social dynamics. Justice must not only be done but seen to be done — for all. While daughters-in-law undoubtedly deserve strong legal protections, this should not come at the cost of denying similar safeguards to others—such as men, their mothers, sisters, and other female relatives—who are often falsely implicated in cases under Sections 498A and the Protection of Women from Domestic Violence Act (PWDVA). There is an emerging need to ensure that laws do not become tools of injustice against others. A mature democracy must evolve laws that are sensitive, equitable, and truly just — not just for one gender, but for all.

The women-centric nature of laws like 498A, PWDVA, and rape provisions in India stems from historical gender inequalities, socio-cultural realities, and political imperatives. While these laws have been critical in addressing systemic violence and discrimination against women, their perceived bias has sparked debates about fairness and misuse. Resistance to gender-neutral reforms from women's NGOs, feminists, and government bodies reflects concerns about diluting protections for women in a patriarchal society. However, the growing call for gender neutrality highlights the need for a balanced approach that upholds justice for all, regardless of gender.

The Indian government faces the complex task of reconciling these competing interests. A potential solution lies in amending existing laws to include gender-neutral provisions where appropriate, coupled with stricter mechanisms to prevent misuse. Such reforms would honour India's constitutional commitment to equality while addressing the evolving dynamics of gender relations in the 21st century. Only through inclusive dialogue and evidence-based policymaking can India craft a legal framework that truly treats all as equal in the eyes of the law.

The Silence of Men

A Society That Punishes Empathy for Its Own

In India, and across much of the world, men are expected to be protectors, providers, and silent sufferers. Behind the curtain of gender equality movements and discussions about women's rights—many of which are necessary and noble—lurks an unsettling truth that society has largely chosen to ignore: the suffering of men, especially within the institution of marriage, often goes unacknowledged, unnoticed, and unheard.

A troubling pattern has emerged where men face significant distress in marital disputes, often leading to dire consequences such as suicide and, in some cases, murder. According to data from the National Crime Records Bureau (NCRB), married men have a significantly higher suicide rate than women, with marriage-related issues accounting for a notable portion of these deaths. Estimates suggest that around 600 men, primarily husbands, are murdered annually by their wives or their families, often in circumstances tied to marital discord or false legal cases. Yet, despite the awareness among scholars, dignitaries, and even the general public, there is a conspicuous silence surrounding these issues.

According to available data and legal commentaries, nearly three times more men commit suicide due to marital issues than women in India. Reports and activist groups allege that over 600 men are murdered by their wives or driven to death each year, yet such claims rarely make headlines or spark outrage. False cases—be it of dowry harassment, domestic violence, or Section 498A abuse—have torn apart countless families, leaving men stigmatized, imprisoned without evidence, and shamed without trial. Yet, public discourse around these issues remains disturbingly quiet.

Why this deafening silence?

The most tragic irony is that men, too, have become complicit in this silence. Influential personalities, celebrities, scholars, and even men's peers often refrain from addressing men's issues publicly. Why? The answer is layered with social fear, gender politics, and an ingrained cultural narrative that equates masculinity with invulnerability.

One phrase that captures this paradox well is: "Every man is a feminist till he meets his wife in family court." It's not an attack on feminism but a commentary on selective empathy and the performative nature of modern gender discourse. Many men parrot feminist lines to appear progressive or respectful—until they find themselves on the receiving end of a weaponized legal system. Then, they discover how society is not equally empathetic to both genders.

What are they afraid of?

For many men, speaking out means facing social backlash, accusations of misogyny, and professional or personal ostracization. Men who champion men's rights are mocked, dismissed, or even vilified. The fear of being labeled as insensitive, regressive, or anti-women silences even those who have personally suffered. There's a subtle but powerful cultural pressure: *"Real men don't complain. They endure."*

Worse still, men are expected to be protectors of women—even at the cost of their own dignity. When a woman is abused or harassed, men rightfully rally in her defense. But when a man is falsely accused, beaten, emotionally manipulated, or driven to suicide, society meets his pain with indifference—or worse, laughter.

One of the primary reasons for the silence surrounding men's issues is the fear of backlash from a society heavily influenced by feminist narratives. Over the past few decades, feminist movements have successfully highlighted women's issues, such as dowry harassment and domestic violence, leading to the enactment of laws like Section 498A of the Indian Penal Code and the Dowry Prohibition Act. These laws, while intended to protect women, have been criticized for their misuse, with false cases often filed to harass husbands and their families. The Supreme Court itself has acknowledged this misuse, describing it as "legal terrorism" in cases like *Sushil Kumar Sharma* (2005).

However, criticizing these laws or advocating for men's rights risks being labeled as misogynistic or anti-woman, a tag that can ruin reputations and careers.

Dignitaries, scholars, and public figures, including men, often avoid speaking out because they fear being ostracized or accused of undermining women's rights. This fear is compounded by the influence of women's organizations and feminist groups, which have significant sway in shaping public discourse and policy. These groups often frame any discussion of men's issues as an attack on women's progress, creating a zero-sum narrative where advocating for men is seen as diminishing women's rights. As a result, even those aware of the alarming statistics—such as the fact that men account for roughly three times more suicides due to marital issues—choose silence over risking their social standing

The Feminist Bias in Public Discourse

The prioritization of women's issues over men's is deeply rooted in societal and institutional biases. Feminist ideologies, while crucial in addressing historical gender inequalities, have sometimes evolved into a one-sided narrative that portrays women as perpetual victims and men as inherent oppressors. This framing leaves little room for acknowledging men as victims of domestic violence, false accusations, or psychological abuse. For instance, Section 498A, which criminalizes cruelty against women, has no equivalent provision to protect men from similar abuses, reinforcing the notion that men cannot be victims.

Media and public discourse amplify this bias by focusing almost exclusively on women's suffering. Cases of dowry deaths or violence against women receive widespread coverage, while men's suicides or murders linked to marital disputes are rarely highlighted. For example, the tragic case of Atul Subhash, a Bengaluru techie who died by suicide in 2024, alleging harassment and false cases by his wife, sparked a brief debate but was quickly overshadowed by counter-narratives dismissing men's rights claims as exaggerated. Women's organizations often justify their focus by citing statistics like the 6,450 dowry-related murders of women in 2022, ignoring the fact that men's suicides and murders also stem from systemic issues. This selective outrage creates a perception that men's suffering is less valid or deserving of sympathy

Why Men Stay Silent: Internalized Expectations and Lack of Solidarity

Men's silence on their own issues is also a product of internalized societal expectations. Traditional gender roles dictate that men must be stoic, resilient, and self-reliant, discouraging them from expressing vulnerability or seeking support. Men facing false accusations or harassment often internalize their distress, leading to severe mental health issues, including depression and suicidality. The lack of institutional support—such as helplines or counseling centers specifically for men—exacerbates this isolation. Organizations like *MyNation Hope Foundation* have noted that men often blame themselves for their family's misery, sometimes believing that suicide will end their loved ones' suffering.

Moreover, men lack the collective solidarity that women's movements have cultivated. While women's organizations like the National Commission for Women (NCW) actively advocate for female victims, there is no equivalent body for men. Proposals for a National Commission for Men have been met with resistance or indifference. Those who support and speak for men face ridicule or dismissal, even from other men, who may view such advocacy as a sign of weakness or an affront to traditional masculinity. This lack of support leaves men feeling abandoned, with many choosing silence over the risk of being labeled as "spineless" or "henpecked."

The Double Standard: Sympathy for Women, Indifference for Men

The stark contrast in societal reactions to male and female victims is a glaring double standard. When a woman is harassed or killed, it triggers widespread outrage, media campaigns, and swift legal action. However, when a man is abused, tortured, or driven to suicide, the response is often muted. This disparity stems from the perception that men are inherently stronger and less deserving of empathy. Even in cases where men are murdered by their wives, such as the estimated 600 annual cases, the narrative often shifts to justify the woman's actions or downplay the crime.

This indifference is not just societal but also institutional. Family courts, police, and the judiciary are often criticized for being biased against men, presuming their guilt in cases of false accusations.

The Consequences of Silence: Emboldening False Claims

The silence of men and society at large has emboldened some women and women's organizations to exploit gender-biased laws without fear of accountability. The low conviction rates under Section 498A—due to difficulties in proving mental cruelty or false claims—mean that many cases are filed as leverage in divorce or property disputes, with little consequence for misuse. This has led to a cycle where false cases proliferate, further eroding trust in the legal system and driving men to despair.

This culture of silence is not just unjust—it is dangerous. It emboldens those who exploit the legal and emotional leverage given to women under the guise of protection. It reinforces the belief that male suffering is either deserved or irrelevant. And it creates a generation of men who are too afraid to even support those brave enough to speak up for them.

The longer men stay silent—either out of fear, shame, or social pressure—the bolder and more unaccountable certain segments of women's rights activism become. This is not a battle of sexes; it's a battle for justice. A society that refuses to acknowledge the pain of half its population cannot claim to be progressive.

Reclaiming the Voice

It's time to reject the narrative that paints male advocacy as misogyny. It's time to support balanced discussions that include men's rights, mental health, and legal protections. And most importantly, it's time for men to find their voice—not in opposition to women, but in pursuit of fairness.

Men must also overcome their reluctance to speak out, recognizing that vulnerability is not weakness but a step toward change. By challenging the narrative that paints them as perpetual oppressors, men can build solidarity and demand empathy for their struggles. Only through collective action and open dialogue can society move beyond the double standards that leave men voiceless and suffering in silence.

In conclusion, the silence on men's issues in India is not just a failure of courage but a reflection of deep-seated biases and systemic inequities. It is time to listen to the cries of men like Atul Subhash and countless others who have been driven to the edge by marital disputes and false cases. Their pain is real, their lives matter, and their voices deserve to be heard.

Because silence is not strength. Strength is standing up for the truth—even when it's unpopular.

Men who remain silent, turn a blind eye and ignore the harassment, legal and emotional abuse faced by other men are greater enemies to justice than even the most radical feminists.

Solution

Gender-Neutral Laws.

Fairness Builds Credibility

When laws are perceived as fair to all genders, they gain more legitimacy and public support. Gender-neutral laws reinforce the idea that justice is not about favouring one group, but about protecting everyone from abuse, discrimination, and violence. This fairness makes it easier for genuinely aggrieved women to come forward without the law being viewed skeptically or as a weapon of misuse.

Protects All, Including Women

Gender-neutral doesn't mean ignoring women's issues. It means the law is worded in a way that protects anyone who is a victim — including women, men, LGBTQ+ individuals, and children. It doesn't reduce the protection women get; it just ensures no one else is excluded.

For example:

A gender-neutral domestic violence law still helps a woman facing abuse — just as it would help a man or trans person in the same situation.

Prevents Backlash Against Women's Rights

When laws are seen as biased or open to misuse, it can create resentment and social backlash — which ironically weakens the cause of women's empowerment. Gender-neutrality reduces the perception of favouritism and promotes unity in fighting injustice, regardless of gender.

Encourages Shared Responsibility

Empowering women is not just about protecting them — it's about creating a society where both genders share responsibility for safety, parenting, earning, and emotional labour. Gender-neutral laws promote this shared responsibility and reflect a more modern, egalitarian society.

Helps Address New-Age Challenges

In today's world, where women are leaders, entrepreneurs, soldiers, and CEOs, the law must also evolve. Gender-neutral laws acknowledge that power dynamics are no longer always skewed in the same direction and that abuse, manipulation, or injustice can happen in any configuration.

Bottom Line:

Yes, it is possible — and desirable — to empower women through gender-neutral laws. The key is ensuring such laws are implemented with sensitivity

to context, strong safeguards, and support systems
(like legal aid, shelters, education, and awareness
campaigns) that make sure women still get the help
they need, while not denying others their right to
justice.

Gender-neutral laws are ultimate fear of Feminists, for
feminist groups, women-centric NGOs, and women's
ministries, the idea of gender-neutral laws is met with
resistance. This is because such laws challenge the
long-held narrative that only women are victims in
domestic and marital issues. When National Crime
Records Bureau (NCRB) data consistently shows that
more men die by suicide due to marital problems, that
increasing numbers of men are reporting domestic
abuse, and that maintenance and child custody laws
are often misused as tools of coercion — the demand
for neutrality becomes harder to ignore. Gender-
neutral laws threaten to expose the imbalance and
misuse within the current system, making it difficult
to justify one-sided policies or secure funding based
solely on a victimhood narrative.

Feminists worst fear - Gender-Neutral Laws

Victimhood

The feminist narrative of victimhood has long been a cornerstone of advocacy for women's rights, particularly in the context of gender-based violence and discrimination. This narrative has emphasized women as primary victims of systemic oppression, often leveraging emotional appeals and selective data to secure funding, policy reforms, and societal support. However, the introduction of gender-neutral laws, coupled with increasing efforts to collect and analyse data on male victims, is challenging this framework. These changes are exposing gaps in the feminist narrative, forcing advocates to justify their claims, and potentially reshaping the allocation of resources previously dominated by women-centric initiatives. This essay explores how gender-neutral laws disrupt the feminist narrative of victimhood, impact funding dynamics, and reveal the strategic use of data suppression, particularly in the context of India's National Crime Records Bureau (NCRB) statistics.

In recent years, there has been growing demand for gender-neutral laws, especially in areas like domestic violence, sexual harassment, and abuse. This shift seeks to ensure legal protection for all individuals—regardless of gender—who may be victims of violence or exploitation. While the intention is to promote equality and fairness, the move toward gender-neutrality has stirred considerable debate, particularly among feminist circles. Some argue that such laws threaten to dilute the hard-earned progress in protecting women, while others see it as a necessary step toward genuine equality.

Gender-Neutral Laws and the Feminist Narrative

Gender-neutral laws aim to treat individuals equally under the legal system, regardless of sex or gender, by avoiding assumptions about roles or victimhood based on gender identity. These laws challenge the feminist narrative, which often portrays women as inherently vulnerable and men as perpetrators. For instance, feminist advocacy has historically focused on women as victims of domestic violence, sexual assault, and other crimes, framing these issues as gendered phenomena rooted in patriarchal structures. While this perspective has driven significant legal protections, such as India's Protection of Women from Domestic Violence Act (2005) and Section 498A of the Indian Penal Code, it has also side-lined male victims and perpetuated a one-dimensional view of gender dynamics.

The push for gender-neutral laws, particularly in areas like domestic violence and sexual assault, disrupts this narrative by acknowledging that men can also be victims. For example, studies and anecdotal evidence suggest that men experience domestic abuse, emotional manipulation, and false accusations, yet these cases are often underreported or dismissed due to societal stigma and legal biases.

Gender-neutral laws, by recognizing male victimhood, challenge the feminist claim that violence is predominantly a women's issue, forcing advocates to confront data that contradicts their narrative. This shift undermines the emotional "sob stories" that have been effective in rallying support, as it becomes harder to portray women as the sole victims in need of protection.

Challenging the Traditional Narrative

Feminist advocacy has long emphasized the victimhood of women, drawing attention to systemic abuse, discrimination, and violence. This narrative has been crucial in securing protective legislation and funding for women-centric programs. However, the introduction of gender-neutral laws brings a broader perspective, compelling institutions to collect and analyse data on male victims and other gender identities.

This data has the potential to reveal that victimhood is not exclusively a female experience. Men, too, may suffer domestic violence, sexual assault, and emotional abuse—though often in silence due to social stigma. As male victimization gains visibility through objective data, it challenges the previously dominant narrative, prompting a re-evaluation of who needs protection and support.

Impact on Funding Dynamics

Feminist organizations have historically secured substantial funding by emphasizing women's victimhood, often at the expense of broader gender equality initiatives. For instance, global funding for gender-based violence programs, such as those supported by UN Women, overwhelmingly targets women and girls, with only 5% of OECD funding allocated to civil society organizations, and an even smaller fraction reaching local women's rights groups. This funding model relies on narratives that highlight women's suffering, often side-lining issues like male suicide, workplace harassment, or custodial violence, which receive less attention and resources.

Gender-neutral laws threaten this funding monopoly by broadening the scope of victimhood. As legal frameworks begin to recognize male victims, funding agencies may redirect resources to address a more inclusive range of issues. For example, if domestic violence laws become gender-neutral, shelters and support services for male victims could receive funding, reducing the share available for women-centric programs. This shift forces feminist organizations to compete for resources in a landscape where their narrative of exclusive victimhood is less compelling. Moreover, the inclusion of men in victim support programs may dilute the perceived urgency of women-centric initiatives, as policymakers and donors prioritize equitable resource distribution.

One significant consequence of this shift is the potential redistribution of funding. Historically, most state and NGO funding has been directed toward women's welfare, based on the presumption of their disproportionate vulnerability. Gender-neutral laws require service providers and governments to recognize other victims as well, possibly dividing existing resources.

For some feminist organizations, this redistribution may be seen as a threat. They may feel the need to defend their cause more aggressively or justify their continued funding by showing measurable outcomes or relevance in a changing landscape. Critics have argued that, in the past, some groups resisted the inclusion of male statistics in crime records (such as India's NCRB—National Crime Records Bureau) precisely to maintain a dominant narrative that supports exclusive funding for women's causes.

The Role of NCRB Data and Suppression of Men's Statistics

In India, the NCRB plays a critical role in shaping perceptions of crime and victimhood through its annual reports. Historically, NCRB data has focused heavily on crimes against women, such as dowry deaths (8,455 cases in 2014) and cruelty by husbands or relatives (122,877 cases in 2014), reinforcing the feminist narrative of women as primary victims. However, critics argue that this focus is partly due to the deliberate exclusion or underreporting of men's victimization, particularly in cases of domestic violence, false accusations, or suicides driven by gender-specific pressures.

Feminist advocacy has often opposed the inclusion of men's statistics in NCRB reports, claiming that it would "dilute" women-centric laws and divert attention from women's issues. For instance, when proposals for gender-neutral laws or data collection on male victims arise, feminist groups argue that such measures undermine the hard-won protections for women. This resistance suggests a strategic effort to maintain the narrative of exclusive victimhood, as comprehensive data on male victims could reveal a more balanced picture of gender-based violence. For example, studies outside India indicate that men constitute a significant portion of domestic violence victims in some contexts, yet this data is rarely reflected in NCRB reports due to societal and legal biases that discourage men from reporting.

The suppression of men's statistics has allowed feminist organizations to dominate funding and policy discussions by presenting skewed data that emphasizes women's suffering. However, as gender-neutral laws gain traction and public awareness of male victimhood grows, pressure is mounting to include men's statistics in NCRB reports. This shift could expose the extent to which feminist narratives have relied on selective data, forcing advocates to justify their claims with more rigorous evidence rather than emotional appeals.

Justifying the Narrative in a Data-Driven Era

As data on male victims becomes more accessible, feminist organizations face the challenge of justifying their narrative of victimhood. The traditional reliance on "crying" or emotional storytelling—while effective in the past—loses potency when confronted with empirical evidence of male victimization. For instance, if NCRB data begins to reflect significant numbers of male victims of domestic violence or false accusations under laws like Section 498A, feminist groups will need to address why their advocacy has overlooked these issues. This scrutiny could weaken their moral authority and public support, as people begin to question the fairness of women-centric laws that exclude men.

Moreover, the rise of men's rights movements and social media platforms like Twitter/X has amplified calls for gender-neutral policies, further challenging feminist narratives. Posts on Twitter/X often highlight cases of men falsely accused of crimes or denied justice, gaining traction among audiences skeptical of feminist claims. These narratives, while sometimes anecdotal, contribute to a growing demand for transparency in crime statistics and legal reforms that address all victims, regardless of gender.

The Fear of Dilution

Another concern frequently raised is that gender-neutral laws may "dilute" the effectiveness of women-centric legislation. Feminist groups often argue that laws were crafted specifically to address the unique vulnerabilities women face, and generalizing them may reduce their efficacy. For instance, laws addressing domestic abuse or workplace harassment were designed with women's experiences in mind, including the power dynamics and cultural stigmas they often face.

However, critics counter that true equality cannot be achieved through selective empathy. If laws are truly just, they must serve all victims, irrespective of gender. Protecting women should not require ignoring the suffering of men or others. The idea that laws should only centre women to be effective inherently undermines the principles of fairness and inclusivity.

Broader Implications and the Path Forward

The shift toward gender-neutral laws and inclusive data collection has profound implications for gender equality. On one hand, it promotes a more equitable legal system that recognizes the complexity of victimhood, acknowledging that both men and women can suffer from violence and discrimination. On the other hand, it challenges feminist organizations to adapt their advocacy to a changing landscape where exclusive narratives of victimhood are less sustainable. Rather than resisting gender-neutral laws or data inclusion, feminist groups could embrace a broader vision of gender equality that addresses the needs of all victims, thereby strengthening their credibility and impact.

To achieve this, several steps are necessary. First, the NCRB should prioritize comprehensive data collection that includes male victims of gender-based violence, ensuring that statistics reflect the full spectrum of victimization. Second, policymakers should engage in balanced discussions about gender-neutral laws, avoiding knee-jerk opposition from any group. Finally, funding agencies should allocate resources based on evidence of need, rather than narratives that prioritize one gender over another. These measures would foster a more inclusive approach to gender justice, reducing the reliance on divisive narratives and promoting fairness.

Conclusion

Gender-neutral laws are reshaping the feminist narrative of victimhood by highlighting the experiences of male victims and challenging the exclusivity of women-centric advocacy. As data on male victimization becomes more visible, feminist organizations face pressure to justify their claims, risking a reduction in funding and influence. The historical suppression of men's statistics in NCRB reports has bolstered feminist narratives but is increasingly unsustainable in a data-driven era. By embracing gender-neutral laws and inclusive data collection, society can move toward a more equitable approach to addressing gender-based violence, one that recognizes the suffering of all victims and allocates resources based on evidence rather than emotional appeals. This shift, while disruptive, offers an opportunity to build a fairer and more transparent framework for gender justice.

The rise of gender-neutral laws represents a pivotal shift in the legal and social landscape. While it may challenge traditional feminist narratives and redistribute resources, it also offers an opportunity to build a more inclusive and data-driven approach to justice. Rather than viewing this shift as a threat, feminist movements could evolve to advocate for all victims, regardless of gender, while continuing to highlight the unique struggles women face. True equity is not a zero-sum game; expanding protection and recognition for all can elevate society as a whole.

Gender-Neutral Laws is not dilution

Strengthening Equality Vs. Women-Centric laws

The call for gender-neutral laws in India has sparked debates about whether such reforms would undermine the protections enshrined in women-centric laws, which were designed to address systemic gender inequalities. Critics argue that transitioning to gender-neutral legislation risks diluting the hard-won rights of women, particularly in a society where patriarchal norms continue to perpetuate violence and discrimination against them. However, this perspective overlooks the potential of gender-neutral laws to complement and expand existing protections, ensuring inclusivity, addressing modern gender complexities, and fostering equitable legal frameworks. This essay argues that, from the perspective of Indian law, gender-neutral laws do not dilute women-centric protections but instead enhance them by broadening their scope, accommodating intersectional identities, and promoting equality without compromising the safeguards women need.

The Role and Importance of Women-Centric Laws in India

India's legal framework includes several women-centric laws enacted to counter deeply entrenched gender inequalities. Statutes such as the Protection of

Women from Domestic Violence Act, 2005 (PWDVA), the Dowry Prohibition Act, 1961, and provisions under the Indian Penal Code (IPC), such as Section 498A (cruelty by husband or his relatives), were designed to address issues like domestic violence, dowry-related abuse, and sexual offences that disproportionately affect women. The Sexual Harassment of Women at Workplace (Prevention, Prohibition and Redressal) Act, 2013 (POSH Act) further protects women from workplace harassment, acknowledging their vulnerability in professional settings. These laws were critical responses to India's patriarchal social structure, where women have historically faced systemic discrimination, violence, and economic exclusion.

The impact of these laws has been significant. For instance, the PWDVA provides women with legal recourse against domestic abuse, including protection orders, monetary relief, and residence rights. Section 498A has been a powerful tool to deter dowry-related cruelty, with over 1 lakh cases registered annually, as per the National Crime Records Bureau (NCRB, 2022). However, these laws are often narrowly tailored, focusing exclusively on women as victims and, in some cases, excluding others who face similar harms, such as men, transgender individuals, or non-binary persons. This limitation has prompted discussions about adopting gender-neutral laws to create a more inclusive legal framework.

The Case for Gender-Neutral Laws in India

Gender-neutral laws aim to protect individuals from harm or discrimination based on universal principles rather than gender-specific criteria. Far from diluting women-centric laws, they can strengthen India's legal system by addressing gaps, promoting inclusivity, and adapting to evolving societal norms. Below are key reasons why gender-neutral laws align with India's constitutional ethos and enhance, rather than undermine, existing protections for women.

India has made significant strides in protecting and empowering women through a robust legal framework aimed at addressing systemic inequalities, gender-based violence, and discrimination. Laws such as the Protection of Women from Domestic Violence Act, 2005, Section 498A of the IPC, and The Sexual Harassment of Women at Workplace (Prevention, Prohibition and Redressal) Act, 2013, among others, reflect the country's commitment to upholding women's rights. However, in recent years, there has been growing discourse around making certain laws gender-neutral. This shift is sometimes perceived as a dilution of women-centric protections. However, from a legal, constitutional, and societal standpoint, gender-neutral laws are not a dilution of women-centric laws, but rather a necessary evolution of the justice system to ensure equality for all citizens as enshrined in the Constitution of India.

Broadening the Scope of Protections

Gender-neutral laws expand the reach of protections to all victims, regardless of gender, without diminishing the remedies available to women. For instance, domestic violence is often perceived as a women-centric issue, but men and transgender individuals also face abuse in domestic settings. A 2018 study by the NGO Men's Rights Association found that 1 in 5 male respondents in urban India reported experiencing domestic abuse, yet they lack legal recourse due to the gender-specific framing of the PWDVA. Making domestic violence laws gender-neutral would ensure that all victims, including women, men, and transgender persons, have access to justice, shelters, and support systems.

Similarly, sexual offence laws under the IPC, such as Section 375 (rape), are women-centric, defining rape as an act committed by a man against a woman. This excludes male and transgender victims of sexual violence, who face significant stigma and legal barriers. The Justice Verma Committee (2013) recommended gender-neutral provisions for sexual offences, noting that such reforms would not weaken protections for women but would ensure justice for all victims. By focusing on the harm rather than the gender of the victim, gender-neutral laws maintain robust protections for women while extending them to others.

Addressing Intersectionality and Gender Diversity

India's recognition of transgender rights, particularly through the NALSA judgment (2014) and the

Transgender Persons (Protection of Rights) Act, 2019, underscores the need for laws that account for diverse gender identities. Women-centric laws, while essential, may inadvertently exclude non-binary, transgender, or gender-nonconforming individuals who face similar forms of discrimination or violence. Gender-neutral laws are better equipped to address intersectional identities, ensuring protections for individuals who experience harm based on gender identity, caste, religion, or disability.

For example, a gender-neutral workplace harassment law could protect cisgender women from sexual harassment, transgender women from gender-based discrimination, and men from hostile work environments, all within a single framework. This inclusivity aligns with Article 15 of the Indian Constitution, which prohibits discrimination on grounds of sex, and Article 14, which guarantees equality before the law. By addressing the diverse realities of gender-based harm, gender-neutral laws strengthen the legal system's ability to deliver justice without diluting women's protections.

Challenging Stereotypes and Promoting Constitutional Equality

Women-centric laws, while necessary to address historical inequalities, can sometimes reinforce stereotypes about women as inherently vulnerable or in need of special protection. Gender-neutral laws challenge these assumptions by framing protections in terms of universal human rights, aligning with India's constitutional commitment to equality. For instance, gender-neutral parental leave policies under the Maternity Benefit (Amendment) Act, 2017, could encourage shared caregiving responsibilities, reducing the burden on women and challenging workplace biases against mothers. A 2021 study by the Centre for Policy Research found that such policies in India increased female workforce participation by 12% in firms adopting flexible leave structures.

Moreover, gender-neutral laws can address misuse concerns associated with women-centric laws, such as false cases under Section 498A, which have been criticized for targeting men unfairly (as noted in judicial observations like Sushil Kumar Sharma v. Union of India, 2005). By focusing on evidence of harm rather than gender, gender-neutral laws promote fairness, reduce backlash against women-centric laws, and maintain their credibility, ensuring continued protection for genuine victims.

Preserving and Complementing Women-Centric Laws

The adoption of gender-neutral laws does not necessitate the repeal of women-centric laws. Instead, these frameworks can coexist, with gender-neutral laws addressing universal harms and women-centric laws tackling issues unique to women, such as reproductive rights or dowry-related abuse. For example, while a gender-neutral domestic violence law could protect all victims, provisions like maternity benefits or protections against female foeticide (under the Pre-Conception and Pre-Natal Diagnostic

Techniques Act, 1994) would remain women-specific, addressing biological and social realities.

The Indian judiciary has already taken steps toward gender neutrality in certain contexts. In Anuj Garg v. Hotel Association of India (2008), the Supreme Court emphasized that laws must evolve to reflect equality principles, striking down gender-specific restrictions that perpetuated stereotypes. Similarly, the decriminalization of Section 377 (IPC) in Navtej Singh Johar v. Union of India (2018) expanded protections against sexual violence to include all genders, demonstrating that gender-neutral reforms can enhance justice without undermining existing rights.

Constitutional Mandate for Equality

The Indian Constitution guarantees equality before the law and equal protection of the laws under Article 14. It also prohibits discrimination on the basis of sex under Article 15. While Article 15(3) permits the state to make special provisions for women and children, it does not preclude the state from addressing the needs and rights of men, transgender persons, and others in vulnerable positions. Gender-neutral laws thus do not conflict with constitutional protections for women; rather, they uphold the broader constitutional vision of equality and non-discrimination for all.

Gender-Neutrality Does Not Erase Gender-Specific Realities

Opponents of gender-neutral reforms often express concern that such changes would ignore the specific, disproportionate harm faced by women in India. This concern is valid and must be acknowledged. However, gender neutrality in law does not imply gender blindness. Legal provisions can still account for the differential impact of certain offences on women. For example, laws can remain sensitive in implementation while maintaining a gender-neutral language. A gender-neutral sexual harassment law, for instance, could still contain guidelines that address the specific vulnerabilities women face at workplaces, while also extending protection to men, transgender, and non-binary individuals who face similar abuse.

Expanding Protection Without Diluting Existing Safeguards

Creating gender-neutral laws does not mean dismantling existing women-centric frameworks. Instead, it involves broadening the scope to include all potential victims and perpetrators. For example, domestic violence, which is currently addressed through a gender-specific lens under the Protection of Women from Domestic Violence Act, has seen increasing instances of men and LGBTQ+ individuals reporting abuse. By extending protections without taking away existing ones, the state can provide a more inclusive justice system without reducing safeguards for women.

India can also take cues from global best practices. Many democratic nations such as the UK, Canada, and Australia have implemented gender-neutral sexual assault and domestic violence laws while continuing to recognize the heightened vulnerabilities of women in policy and judicial interpretation.

The Need for Legal Recognition of All Victims

The Indian legal system must recognize that men and LGBTQ+ persons can also be victims of domestic violence, sexual harassment, and other gendered crimes. The National Crime Records Bureau does not adequately record data on male or LGBTQ+ victims, which creates a gap in policymaking and justice delivery. Laws that are gender-specific may inadvertently deny access to justice for non-female victims or stigmatize their experiences. Creating gender-neutral provisions helps to remove these barriers without diminishing the focus on women's safety.

The Judiciary's Progressive Stand

Indian courts have increasingly adopted a progressive interpretation of gender and justice. In Navtej Singh Johar v. Union of India (2018), the Supreme Court decriminalized homosexuality and emphasized the importance of recognizing the dignity and rights of LGBTQ+ individuals. In National Legal Services Authority (NALSA) v. Union of India (2014), the apex court recognized the rights of transgender individuals and affirmed their right to self-identify their gender. These judgments underline the need for our laws to move beyond the binary and reflect the lived realities of all citizens.

Addressing Concerns About Dilution

Critics of gender-neutral laws argue that they may divert resources or attention from women, who remain disproportionately affected by gender-based violence and discrimination. However, this concern can be addressed through careful legislative design. Gender-neutral laws can include provisions to prioritize funding for women-specific programs, such as shelters or helplines, while extending legal protections to others. Additionally, robust implementation mechanisms, such as gender-sensitized training for law enforcement and judiciary, can ensure that women's needs remain central to the application of gender-neutral laws.

Another concern is that gender-neutral laws may fail to account for the power imbalances inherent in a patriarchal society. To counter this, laws can incorporate affirmative measures, such as enhanced penalties for crimes targeting marginalized groups, including women, or mandatory gender audits to monitor their impact. These strategies ensure that gender-neutral laws uphold the spirit of women-centric protections while embracing inclusivity.

Conclusion

In the Indian legal context, gender-neutral laws do not dilute women-centric protections but rather enhance them by creating a more inclusive, equitable, and constitutionally aligned framework. By broadening the scope of protections, addressing intersectional and diverse gender identities, challenging stereotypes, and complementing existing laws, gender-neutral reforms strengthen India's commitment to equality under Articles 14 and 15 of the Constitution. Far from undermining women's rights, such laws ensure that the legal system evolves to meet the needs of all individuals while preserving the hard-won safeguards for women. Through thoughtful design and implementation, India can embrace gender-neutral laws as a progressive step toward a more just and inclusive society, without compromising the protections women need to thrive.

In conclusion, the move toward gender-neutral laws in India is not a dilution of women-centric protections—it is an expansion of justice. It aligns with the constitutional vision of equality and responds to the evolving understanding of gender, identity, and victimhood. Women-centric laws remain crucial in addressing structural inequalities, but inclusivity should not be seen as a threat. Instead, India's legal system must evolve to serve all citizens equitably, without sacrificing the protections that women continue to need. Gender-neutral laws represent not a rollback of progress, but a step forward in ensuring that no victim is left unheard or unprotected.

State sponsored Legal Terrorism

The suffering of the martyrs is often described as persecution, which can encompass oppression, false accusation, and torture. The specific term depends on the context:

Persecution: Systematic mistreatment, often due to religious, political, or ideological beliefs, including imprisonment, torture, or execution.

Oppression: Prolonged, unjust treatment or control, often by a governing authority, which may include denying rights or freedoms. This is a broader term that includes unjust treatment, often by those in power. If a martyr suffers under a regime or group that punishes them for their beliefs or identity, this can be called oppression.

False Accusation: Wrongful charges or blame, often used to justify punishment or martyrdom. This refers specifically to being wrongly blamed or charged. Many martyrs have faced false accusations as part of their persecution

Torture: This is the physical or psychological pain inflicted deliberately, often a method used against the martyrs to force them to recant or as punishment.

Deliberate infliction of physical or psychological pain, commonly associated with martyrdom in historical or religious contexts.

Promoters of Legal Terrorism.

The phrase "Let men suffer" is attributed to Chowdhury, former Minister of State, In a 2006 interview. During discussions about the Protection of Women from Domestic Violence Act, 2005, Chowdhury was questioned about potential misuse of the law against men. In response, she remarked, "That's not a bad idea except I have such pity for men," and emphasized, "Any law is better than no law at all" when it comes to protecting women.

If a minister openly advocates for men to suffer as a consequence of false accusations under Section 498A IPC, domestic violence, or rape cases—where men are tortured, oppressed, and persecuted—many are forced to pay exorbitant sums, often their lifelong savings, sometimes for a marriage that lasted just a day. Others face parental alienation or are blackmailed over child visitation or custody. For some men, this becomes unbearable mental torture, pushing them to take extreme steps, including ending their own lives.

Also In another statement aimed at empowering women, former minister Chowdhury urged Indian women not to blindly trust their husbands, especially when it comes to protecting themselves from HIV/AIDS. Highlighting the risk posed by unfaithful partners, she advised women to take charge of their own safety by keeping condoms at home, suggesting that husbands could bring the virus back after visiting other women. Chowdhury, known for her outspoken views, challenged societal discomfort around the topic, saying, "We are so embarrassed to ask about condoms. Women need to get condoms to protect themselves—let the men be suspicious." She added, "Men will not buy a condom when they come staggering home while drunk," she not only accused Men as sex addicts, visiting Brothels, alcoholic and come home and Rape their Women again.

Maneka Gandhi, former Union Minister for Women and Child Development, made the statement "*All violence is male-generated*" during a live Facebook interaction on September 14, 2015, as part of the ministry's #100Women initiative. The comment was in response to a question about gender sensitization, where she emphasized the critical role of men in addressing violence, stating, "The role of men in gender sensitization was the most critical since all the violence is male-generated."

Minister generalized men as the sole perpetrators of violence and overlooked violence by women. They cited cases like domestic violence against men and rising male suicide rates, claiming the remark was insensitive and biased, However, she did not explicitly address female-perpetrated violence in this statement, leading to accusations of a one-sided perspective, terming All women are Victims and All men are perpetrators.

The statement reflects one sided biased advocacy and was criticized for its sweeping generalization, especially given evidence like NCRB data showing women contributing to crimes (e.g., 10–40% of murder/attempted murder charges from 2001–2013) and studies indicating women's role in domestic violence. Without a primary source clarifying her intent.

The recent ruling by the Supreme Court has raised concerns about how adultery may be indirectly legitimized within the framework of marriage. According to the judgment, if a marriage between a man and a woman is subsisting and they had access to each other, the husband will be presumed to be the legal father of any child born during that time—even if the wife claims the child was conceived through an adulterous relationship with another man. By not mandating a DNA test to establish paternity in such cases, the ruling is seen by critics as indirectly promoting adultery. It effectively shields the woman from legal consequences of infidelity while potentially compelling the husband to bear financial responsibility—such as child maintenance—for a child to whom he may have no biological connection. This not only raises ethical and legal questions about fairness but also puts the husband in a vulnerable position with limited recourse to challenge paternity.

Similarly, in a recent judgment, a High Court ruled in favor of a married woman who spent the night in a hotel room with another man. The court compared her to Draupadi, portraying her as a victim, without questioning why she was alone with another man without her husband's knowledge. This clearly suggests a relationship between the two, yet the law still protected her interests. Judgments like these may set a precedent that encourages other women to engage in adultery without facing consequences—ultimately at the husband's expense. What if a man stays with another woman and his wife accuses him of adultery—will the law take the same stand?

India continues to uphold traditional values, and practices such as a married woman sharing a room with a stranger or having a child with another man are still widely considered taboo. These ideas, often influenced by Western norms, are not accepted by the majority in Indian society, with only a few feminist voices supporting such notions. Courts should avoid referencing epic stories to justify or portray women solely as victims. Instead, judgments should rely on circumstantial and scientific evidence—such as lie detector tests and DNA analysis—which are standard in many countries around the world. Indian courts should adopt these scientific methods more extensively to establish the truth. For instance, DNA testing should be mandatory in all child support claims, and lie detector tests should be used in cases involving dowry laws (Section 498A IPC), domestic violence, POCSO, rape, and maintenance. This approach would not only help reveal the truth but also deter individuals from filing false cases, ultimately helping to reduce the backlog in the judiciary.

The Invisible Victims

Over the decades, India has taken commendable legal strides to safeguard the rights and dignity of women through strong, women-centric legislation. However, in the name of protecting one gender, the country has inadvertently neglected another. Thousands of men and their families have suffered in silence due to the misuse of certain gender-specific laws, and in the most tragic cases, have ended their lives. This is a crisis that deserves national attention — not as a counter to women's rights, but as a call for justice, compassion, and equality for all.

Laws such as Section 498A of the Indian Penal Code (IPC), which were enacted to protect women from cruelty by husbands and in-laws, have over the years also been misused in many instances. The Supreme Court of India, in multiple rulings, including *Arnesh Kumar v. State of Bihar* (2014), has acknowledged the misuse of this law and the need for safeguards against its arbitrary use. Yet, despite such recognition, legislative reform has been painfully slow.

Every year, thousands of men accused under these laws find themselves imprisoned without trial, lose their jobs, suffer irreparable damage to their reputations, or are pushed to emotional and financial ruin. Families—elderly parents, siblings, and even children—often face social stigma, police harassment, and legal battles for years, sometimes over false or exaggerated allegations. In such circumstances, when men find no legal support system, counselling, or societal understanding, some see no way out but suicide.

According to the National Crime Records Bureau (NCRB), men account for more than 70% of all suicides in India, and a significant portion of these are attributed to "family problems" and "marital issues." Yet, the plight of these men remains largely invisible in public discourse, media coverage, and policy planning.

What makes this crisis more tragic is the government's consistent refusal to consider gender-neutral laws, especially in areas like domestic violence, sexual harassment, and alimony. Ministries dedicated to women's welfare have often opposed such reforms, arguing that gender neutrality would undermine protections for women. While the fear of regression in women's rights is valid, it should not come at the cost of ignoring suffering in another section of society.

The refusal to even acknowledge the suffering of men under these laws, let alone legislate to protect them, is not just indifference—it is a systemic failure. The state is duty-bound to protect all citizens, not just one gender. By failing to provide equal legal protection to men and by resisting reforms that could prevent innocent lives from being destroyed, the state bears moral responsibility for the lives lost to legal misuse and societal neglect.

These men, many of whom were ordinary citizens—sons, fathers, husbands, brothers—have become martyrs to a system that promised justice but delivered silence. Their pain must no longer be ignored or dismissed under the guise of political correctness or gender-based assumptions. Justice that excludes the innocent in the name of protecting the vulnerable is no justice at all.

India needs gender-neutral laws, not because women no longer need protection, but because justice must be blind to gender. It must see only the facts, the suffering, and the humanity of every individual—male, female, or otherwise. The time for reform is not tomorrow, but today.

Why State Sponsored?

When men experience systemic oppression within a relationship, it often goes unnoticed due to the societal narrative that primarily sees men as aggressors and women as victims. However, emotional manipulation, threats, blackmail, and abuse by a spouse can severely affect a man's mental and emotional well-being.

When men experience systemic oppression within a relationship, it often goes unnoticed due to the societal narrative that primarily sees men as aggressors and women as victims. However, emotional manipulation, threats, blackmail, and abuse by a spouse can severely affect a man's mental and emotional well-being.

In cases of false accusations—particularly under laws like Section 498A of the IPC (dowry harassment), domestic violence, or even rape or molestation allegations—a man can be arrested without substantial evidence. These charges, even if proven false later, can destroy his reputation, career, and social relationships. Many such men face public shaming, media trials, and ostracization, leaving them isolated and hopeless.

Torture and persecution—whether emotional (like constant insults, threats, or gas lighting) or legal (such as prolonged court battles, being denied access to their children, or being extorted for large settlements)—can become overwhelming. Parental alienation, where fathers are kept away from their children after separation, is especially heart-breaking and has been linked to severe depression and suicidal ideation.

The stigma around male vulnerability compounds the problem. Many men are socially conditioned to suppress their emotions, and when they do reach out for help, they're often dismissed or mocked. With no support systems, crippling legal battles, and the weight of unjust suffering, some men feel suicide is the only escape from their pain.

Oppression, false accusations, torture, and persecution by wives, particularly in the context of legal and social frameworks in India, can create severe psychological, financial, and social pressures that drive some men to suicide. Below is an exploration of how these factors contribute to male suicide, with a focus on India, drawing on available evidence and socio-cultural dynamics:

In India, men account for approximately 70% of suicides, with over 122,000 male deaths compared to 48,000 female deaths in 2022, a rate nearly three times higher, according to NCRB data. Despite this alarming disparity, the government has been criticized for failing to address male-specific mental health issues or enact laws to protect men from societal pressures, such as financial burdens, marital disputes, or alleged misuse of legal provisions like Section 498A. Men's rights activists argue that this inaction reflects a systemic bias, leaving men vulnerable without adequate support or legal recourse. Some even claim that the state's neglect equates to complicity, labelling these deaths as "**state-sponsored murders**" due to the lack of targeted policies to address the crisis. However, this perspective oversimplifies a complex issue, as suicide prevention requires multifaceted approaches beyond gender-specific legislation.

False Accusations and Legal Misuse

In cases of false accusations—particularly under laws like Section 498A of the IPC (dowry harassment), domestic violence, or even rape or molestation allegations—a man can be arrested without substantial evidence. These charges, even if proven false later, can destroy his reputation, career, and social relationships. Many such men face public shaming, media trials, and ostracization, leaving them isolated and hopeless.

Section 498A of IPC: This law, intended to protect women from cruelty by husbands or in-laws, is mostly misused to falsely accuse men of dowry harassment or domestic violence. Such accusations can lead to immediate arrests without investigation, public humiliation, and prolonged legal battles. Men's rights groups, like the Save Indian Family Foundation, argue that false cases under Section 498A cause significant emotional and financial distress. For example, a 2016 article noted that false dowry complaints can amount to mental cruelty, as seen in court rulings like Sanjay vs. Anita (Bombay High Court), where such actions justified divorce due to the husband's suffering.

Impact: The stigma of being labelled a "dowry offender" or "abuser," combined with job loss, social ostracism, and legal costs, can lead to hopelessness. A 2021 Hindustan Times article reported that around 65,000 married men died by suicide annually compared to 28,000 married women, suggesting a significant burden on men, potentially linked to such legal misuse.

Psychological Torture and Mental Cruelty

Domestic Abuse Against Men: While less reported due to societal stigma, men face psychological abuse, such as public humiliation, insults, or alienation from family, as noted in cases like *Dastane vs. Dastane*, where a wife's harassment led to mental cruelty grounds for divorce. Emotional abuse, including parental alienation (denying access to children), can exacerbate feelings of isolation and worthlessness.

Cultural Barriers: Indian society often dismisses male victims of abuse, as men are expected to be stoic. A 2021 Hindustan Times article highlighted that men rarely report domestic violence due to humiliation and fear of false counter-accusations, increasing their vulnerability to mental health crises.

Suicide Risk: Studies show that psychological distress from domestic violence is a major risk factor for suicide. A Bangalore study found domestic violence as a key contributor to male suicides, with 30–50% of male suicides linked to alcohol abuse, often a coping mechanism for emotional pain.

Financial Oppression and Blackmail:

Extortion via Legal Cases: Men accused under Section 498A or domestic violence laws may face demands for large settlements, sometimes their lifelong savings, to resolve cases, even for short-lived marriages. X posts from 2024–2025 reflect sentiments that men are "trapped" by such laws, leading to financial ruin and despair.

Child Custody and Visitation: Blackmail over child custody or visitation rights adds to mental strain. Men denied access to children or coerced into payments for visitation face parental alienation, which can be an "unbearable mental torture," as noted in user queries. This aligns with research showing family-related stressors, like divorce or separation, increase suicide risk in men.

Economic Burden: A 2015 study on property rights suggested that intra-household conflicts, including financial disputes, can heighten stress and suicide rates for both genders, but men often bear the brunt of economic expectations in patriarchal setups.

Persecution and Social Stigma:

Societal Perception: Men accused of crimes like dowry harassment or rape face social persecution, including loss of reputation and community support. A 2020 study on torture survivors in Nepal (relevant due to cultural similarities) showed that male victims of violence, including false accusations, reported severe emotional pain and social isolation, contributing to long-term mental health issues.

whether emotional (like constant insults, threats, or gaslighting) or legal (such as prolonged court battles, being denied access to their children, or being extorted for large settlements)—can become overwhelming. Parental alienation, where fathers are kept away from their children after separation, is especially heart-breaking and has been linked to severe depression and suicidal ideation.

The stigma around male vulnerability compounds the problem. Many men are socially conditioned to suppress their emotions, and when they do reach out for help, they're often dismissed or mocked. With no support systems, crippling legal battles, and the weight of unjust suffering, some men feel suicide is the only escape from their pain.

Lack of Support: Unlike women, men lack legal protections or social movements addressing their abuse. The absence of gender-neutral laws or support systems, as ighlighted in a 2016 a media article, leaves men vulnerable to unchecked harassment. This isolation is compounded by media portrayals, like those criticized in Satyamev Jayate, which often ignore male victims.

Suicide as an Outcome:

Statistics: India's suicide rate is approximately 10.3 per 100,000, with a male-to-female ratio of 1.4:1. Men aged 15–44 account for 71% of suicides, with young men (15–29) at the highest risk (38 per 100,000). A 2021 study noted that socio-economic stressors, including family disputes and legal issues, are major drivers. A 2024 X post cited 517 male suicides in 2023 linked to domestic violence, mental cruelty, and adultery, underscoring the issue's severity.

Mechanisms: Psychological autopsies reveal that men facing marital discord, false accusations, or financial ruin often develop depression, hopelessness, or substance abuse, all linked to suicide. A Chennai study found 88% of suicides had diagnosable mental disorders, yet only 10% sought mental health support, reflecting stigma around male vulnerability.

Extreme Cases: The pressure of false accusations or torture can push men to view suicide as an escape. For instance, a 2001 study noted that husbands of substance-abusing wives faced high suicide attempt rates due to marital stress, a dynamic that parallels false accusation scenarios.

Critical Perspective:

While the above factors highlight genuine issues, the narrative of male victimhood must be balanced. Women in India face significantly higher rates of domestic violence (33.5% lifetime prevalence per 2005 NFHS-III) and dowry-related deaths (8,391 in 2010). The misuse of laws like Section 498A is debated, with courts dismissing many false cases, but convictions still occur, indicating some validity to claims. The lack of gender-neutral laws, however, amplifies men's vulnerability, as noted by activists. The absence of comprehensive studies specifically linking false accusations by wives to male suicides limits definitive conclusions, but anecdotal evidence and broader suicide research suggest a plausible connection.

Oppression, false accusations, torture, and persecution by wives, often facilitated by legal misuse and societal biases, create a toxic environment for some Indian men, leading to financial ruin, social isolation, and psychological despair. These stressors, combined with a lack of support and stigma around male vulnerability, significantly contribute to male suicides, particularly among young men. Addressing this requires gender-neutral laws, mental health support, and societal acknowledgment of male victims, while continuing to protect women from abuse. For deeper insights, studies like those in The Lancet (2018) on suicide trends or NCRB data (2020) on male suicides can provide further context

Conclusion: Justice Cannot Be Selective

India cannot call itself a just society while it allows one gender to be presumed guilty and the other always presumed victim. Gender justice means equality for all-not privilege for some. The silence of the government is not neutral-it is complicit. And if change doesn't come from the top, it must rise from the ground.

The suffering of men and families affected by the misuse of women-centric biased laws is a tragic reality that underscores the need for gender-neutral reforms in India. While the government and women's ministries have been cautious, their resistance to change does not equate to complicity in a "genocide." Rather, it reflects the challenge of balancing competing priorities in a complex society. By adopting gender-neutral laws with safeguards to prevent misuse and preserve women's protections, India can address the grievances of men without undermining the rights of women. This approach honours the constitutional vision of equality, ensures justice for all, and moves beyond divisive rhetoric to create a legal system that serves every citizen equitably.

If the government and its ministries believe that empowering women can be achieved through biased, women-centric laws at the expense of justice for men, then they must also take responsibility for the consequences and Innocent blood in their hands, including any crimes committed by women or their families by denying justice to men. The government's longstanding inaction may be seen as complicity in what some might describe as systemic harm, potentially state-sponsored injustice.

Furthermore, it is asserted that governmental inaction over several decades implies complicity in these acts, characterizing them as state-sponsored. The perspective implies that gender-biased laws may inadvertently enable the misuse of legal provisions by women, potentially leading to a significant number of male suicides. while also accusing the government of enabling a form of systemic injustice, state sponsored Genocide with Legal terrorism.

Our claim is backed by facts and figures—numbers don't lie. Men die by suicide at three times the rate of women, yet for decades, laws have continued to favor women with gender-specific protections, ignoring the issues men face. This clearly shows that while the government promotes initiatives like **#BetiBachao**, there's no equivalent support like **#BetaBachao**. This reveals a clear bias and a step-motherly approach toward men. No one can stop the government from creating schemes or reservations exclusively for women, but making one-sided laws that favor only women is unethical and unconstitutional, especially when their misuse can destroy men's lives. The government cannot wash its hands of this—it has blood on its hands and is responsible for a silent genocide through what can only be called legal terrorism.

State Sponsored Genocide

When Laws Meant to Protect Become Weapons

In a country where justice is claimed to be blind, men in India are bleeding silently, victims of a legal system that has, in the name of protecting one gender, turned a blind eye to another. For decades, India's women-centric laws—crafted with good intentions—have been misused, abused, and weaponized. Men and their families have paid the price in ruined reputations, destroyed families, mental trauma, and thousands of suicides. Yet, the Indian government, especially the Ministry of Women and Child Development, continues to stonewall demands for gender-neutral laws, making it complicit in this state-sponsored negligence. This isn't just failure—it is betrayal.

The Context of Women-Centric Laws and Their Impact

India's women-centric laws, such as Section 498A of the Indian Penal Code (IPC) (cruelty by husband or his relatives), the Protection of Women from Domestic Violence Act, 2005 (PWDVA), and the Dowry Prohibition Act, 1961, were enacted to address the pervasive issues of domestic violence, dowry-related abuse, and gender inequality in a deeply patriarchal society. These laws have been instrumental in providing women with legal recourse against abuse, with over 1.2 lakh cases registered under Section 498A alone in 2022, according to the National Crime Records Bureau (NCRB). They reflect India's constitutional commitment to equality (Article 15) and the need to protect women from systemic vulnerabilities.

However, critics argue that these laws, particularly Section 498A, are prone to misuse due to their non-bailable and cognizable nature, which allows arrests without preliminary investigation. Reports from men's rights groups, such as Save Indian Family Foundation, claim that false allegations of dowry harassment or cruelty have led to the harassment of men and their families, including elderly parents and siblings. A 2010 study by the Centre for Social Research estimated that 10-15% of Section 498A cases may involve misuse, though hard data on "false" cases is contentious due to varying definitions of misuse. High-profile cases, such as the 2014 suicide of a Bangalore techie, reportedly driven by alleged false dowry accusations, have fuelled narratives of men as victims of legal bias. The despair of such cases has led some to claim that men and their families, pushed to the brink, are "martyrs" of a biased system.

The Human Cost: Suicides and Family Distress

The argument that women-centric laws have contributed to suicides among men and their families is rooted in anecdotal evidence and media reports, though comprehensive data linking suicides directly to legal misuse is scarce. The NCRB reported 1.7 lakh suicides in India in 2022, with men accounting for 71% of cases, but the causes are multifaceted, including financial stress, mental health issues, and family disputes. Men's rights activists argue that the stigma, financial ruin, and social ostracism caused by false accusations under laws like Section 498A exacerbate mental health crises, sometimes leading to suicide. For instance, a 2017 case in Delhi, where a man and his parents took their lives after alleged harassment over dowry accusations, galvanized calls for reform.

These tragedies highlight a critical issue: the legal system's failure to adequately address misuse while protecting genuine victims. The Supreme Court, in cases like *Sushil Kumar Sharma v. Union of India* (2005) and *Arnesh Kumar v. State of Bihar* (2014), has acknowledged the potential for misuse of Section 498A, urging caution in arrests and investigations. Yet, the lack of systemic reforms to prevent abuse of these laws has left many men and their families feeling helpless, fuelling perceptions of injustice.

The Numbers Don't Lie—They Scream

According to the National Crime Records Bureau (NCRB) 2022:

- 1,18,979 men died by suicide due to "family problems" and "marriage-related issues."

- That is nearly 3 times the number of women in the same category.
- Over 72% of all suicides in India are committed by men.

The media, the government, and civil society routinely ignore these horrifying numbers. There are no helplines, no shelters, no commissions, no support systems, and worst of all—no laws that even acknowledge that men or male family members can be victims of abuse, harassment, or legal misuse.

Weaponization of Section 498A IPC

Take Section 498A IPC, a non-bail-able offence designed to protect women from cruelty by the husband or his relatives. What began as a tool for justice has become, in many cases, a tool for revenge.

In 2021, out of 47,952 cases registered under 498A, over 87% ended in acquittals or were dropped.

The Supreme Court of India in *Arnesh Kumar v. State of Bihar* (2014) noted the "legal terrorism" caused by the misuse of this provision.

The Law Commission of India (2003, 2012) and the Justice Malimath Committee Report (2003) both strongly recommended safeguards and gender-neutral frameworks—but their recommendations have been consistently ignored.

So who pays the price for these politically convenient blind spots? Innocent men, elderly parents, unmarried sisters, and even children who get entangled in false cases—lives shattered for years, often with no conviction in sight.

Domestic Violence Law - Mard ko dard nahi hota

The PWDVA, 2005, one of the most cited laws in family disputes, recognizes only women as victims. But where is the protection for:

- Men who are physically abused or mentally harassed by spouses?
- Elderly parents thrown out of their own homes on false domestic violence claims?
- LGBTQ+ individuals in abusive relationships?

There is not a single line in this law that acknowledges the possibility of male or non-female victims. And this is in direct violation of Article 14 of the Indian Constitution, which guarantees equality before the law.

Systemic Neglect by Government and Women's Ministry

What makes this injustice unforgivable is that it is not accidental—it is deliberate and sustained.

The Ministry of Women and Child Development has repeatedly rejected calls for gender-neutral reforms to domestic violence and sexual harassment laws.

Proposals to make sexual harassment laws, rape laws, and marital abuse laws inclusive of male and LGBTQ+ victims have been met with silence or active resistance.

Men's rights activists are vilified, mocked, and dismissed—even as they carry evidence of suicides, police abuse, and legal harassment.

This Is Not Mere Injustice—It Is State Sponsored

When the state allows laws to be abused, refuses to protect the innocent, and actively ignores data that proves the suffering of an entire section of society—it stops being a democracy and starts being an enabler of oppression.

Every man who has been jailed without trial, every elderly parent harassed by police, every boy who has taken his life in despair—are casualties of a system that refused to listen. These are not just unfortunate incidents—they are state sponsored murders. If the government continues to ignore their cries, it carries moral blood on its hands.

What else can you call it but state-sponsored genocide when yearly over 171,000 men have taken their own lives, and the government has done nothing—simply because the cause was related to marital issues and women is reason for these murders?

Men are dying and killed at three times the rate of women, yet they have no laws to protect them, no ministry to turn to for help—while even animals have dedicated ministries.

Every 4.5 minutes, a man ends his life, compared to one woman every seven minutes. Still, the government focuses on laws exclusively for women, offering nothing for men. If this isn't state-sponsored Genocide, then what is?

The government should not further divide the nation based on gender, especially when it has already polarized the country along religious lines as part of its election strategy. The gender narrative has been reduced to a tool for building a women-centric vote bank and fueling profit-driven schemes for ministers and vested interests. It's an open secret where the funds actually go — the extravagant wardrobes, luxury vehicles, expensive fancy dress cloths and lavish lifestyles of ministers cannot possibly be sustained by their official salaries alone. Meanwhile, truly needy women receive little to no support. The policies of the Ministry for Women often feel step-motherly, creating rifts within families — especially between daughters-in-law and their in-laws. In the end, it's a cruel cycle of divide and profit, with the innocent men and his family driven to tragic ends.

Contact and Support

Connect with Author:

Need help?

If you know someone who needs support, simply scan the QR code above and reach out to us.

Bibliography/References

- https://zenodo.org/records/7803874 - GEMS OF JUDGMENTS - PROMOTING LEGAL TERRORISM.
- https://zenodo.org/records/4917024 - SILENCING THE TRUTH - STUDY ON MEN.
- https://zenodo.org/records/4899760 - REFORM THE JUSTICE SYSTEM TO PREVENT FUTURE INJUSTICE.
- https://zenodo.org/records/4688009 - BIAS BY BIRTH-DISCRIMINATION AGAINST MEN
- https://zenodo.org/records/4649599 - MEN'S LIVES MATTERS–SUICIDES BY MEN-STUDY ON MEN'S HEALTH.
- https://zenodo.org/records/4537819 - CRIMES BY INDIAN WOMEN.
- https://zenodo.org/records/4581530 - LEGAL TERRORISM IN MATRIMONIAL DISPUTES-SOLUTION FOR LEGAL TERRORISM
- https://zenodo.org/records/4537819 - CRIMES BY INDIAN WOMEN: A SILENT EPIDEMIC

Author's Bio

Mr. Rudolph Dsouza, a pioneering family rights activist and one of the Earliest founding figures of the Men's Rights movement in India, has made a groundbreaking contribution through his latest study report. With sharp insights and deep compassion for the unseen victims of the legal system, he brings to light the hidden casualties that are often ignored by mainstream narratives.

He was born in Bombay (now Mumbai) and graduated from Mangalore University. He completed his professional training in computer science at IBM, Canada. In addition to being a legal professional, he is the founder of the NGO *MyNation Hope Foundation.* He has authored several scholarly study reports, one of which has been referenced in a gender studies program by UCLA, He is deeply passionate about writing. At just 10 years old, he wrote and published a short poem. During his college years, he went on to write and publish 27 short non-fiction and love stories in his father tongue, Konkani.

His report exposes how a broken legal framework-originally designed to protect-has instead led to the false accusation of countless men. Innocent husbands and fathers have become easy targets under the weight of one-sided, biased laws. Men are not only wrongfully implicated but often subjected to prolonged harassment, social stigma, mental agony, and in extreme cases, driven to death.

Mr. Dsouza also highlights a heart-wrenching consequence rarely discussed: the alienation of fathers from their own children. Legal provisions, meant to address genuine grievances, are increasingly weaponized, tearing apart the bond between a father and his child. Families are not just broken-they are devastated beyond repair, as systemic legal overreach empowers one side while silencing the other.

Through meticulous research, real-world case studies, and an unflinching look at ground realities, Mr. Dsouza's study serves as a clarion call for urgent reforms. His work urges society, policymakers, and judicial institutions to recognize that justice must be balanced - that in the pursuit of protecting one group, we must not unknowingly destroy another. Only by addressing these silent sufferings can India hope to build a truly fair, equitable, and 'Viksit Bharat.'